Kaizen Mindset

Transform Your Life with the Power of Continuous Improvement

Hiroshi Suzuki

Table of Contents

INTRODUCTION

Kaizen is a Japanese word that means "change for the better." "Kaizen Mindset: Transform Your Life with the Power of Continuous Improvement" explores this transformative philosophy. This book provides a thorough manual for applying the ideas of Kaizen to everyday situations, with an emphasis on little adjustments that add up to significant gains. The Kaizen mindset is rooted in Japanese corporate techniques that transformed Toyota's manufacturing system. It promotes continuous improvement over abrupt, irregular changes.

The author examines the psychological and practical underpinnings of Kaizen, showing how this methodology may be used for relationships, personal growth, health, and general well-being in addition to the corporate setting. Readers discover how to pinpoint areas for development, create attainable goals, and maintain momentum over time with the help of helpful advice, real-world examples, and doable actions. The book strongly emphasizes the value of perseverance, consistency, and the compounding effect of tiny, constructive acts.

"Kaizen Mindset" is a comprehensive approach to leading a more contented and well-rounded existence rather than merely an efficiency tactic. It gives readers the confidence to welcome change and encourages a proactive approach to ongoing personal development. This book is an excellent resource for anyone aiming to improve their life and create long-lasting, beneficial changes.

CHAPTER I

The Foundations of Kaizen

History and Roots in Japanese Culture

Translating to "continuous improvement," the Japanese idea of Kaizen has profound cultural origins and has dramatically influenced contemporary management techniques worldwide. Its history is entwined with Japan's post-World War II economic recovery and the nation's cultural emphasis on harmony, discipline, and attention to detail. Examining the industrial, historical, and cultural settings in which Kaizen originated is crucial to comprehending its beginnings and development.

It has long been a cultural value of Japan to encourage steady, incremental improvement. This idea may be observed in many facets of traditional Japanese culture, including the meticulous attention to detail in calligraphy, tea ceremonies, and gardening. The Japanese term "Kaizen" itself is made up of the letters "kai" (change) and "zen" (good), which together represent the idea that changes can be made by making gradual, tiny movements toward a better goal. This cultural environment fostered the growth of Kaizen as an organized method of improvement in an industrial setting.

After World War II, Japan's manufacturing sector formally implemented Kaizen ideas. Japan had difficulty reconstructing its infrastructure and economy after the war's damage. Japanese businesses tried to improve quality and productivity at this time to compete internationally. The introduction of American quality control techniques, especially those promoted by W. Edwards Deming and Joseph M. Juran, who visited Japan in the early 1950s, was one of the significant factors in this change.

Deming and Juran introduced statistical methods for quality control and management strategies, emphasizing the value of incorporating all staff members in the improvement process. The Plan-Do-Check-Act (PDCA) or Deming Cycle paradigm struck a profound chord with Japanese managers and engineers. The notion that quality enhancement has to be an ongoing, iterative process matched Japanese cultural norms and values quite well.

A significant contributor to the creation and spread of Kaizen was Toyota, one of the top automakers in Japan. Toyota created the Toyota Production System (TPS), which incorporated Kaizen ideas into its manufacturing processes under the direction of Taiichi Ohno and Shigeo Shingo. TPS strongly emphasized reducing waste (muda), increasing productivity, and guaranteeing quality throughout the production process. This method transformed Toyota's operations and established a new benchmark for worldwide manufacturing standards.

At Toyota, Kaizen was implemented by giving employees at all levels the authority to spot inefficiencies and recommend changes. This bottom-up strategy was novel at the time and starkly contrasted the top-down management philosophies common in many Western businesses. Toyota's success with Kaizen exemplified how staff participation in ongoing attempts to improve processes may result in better goods, lower costs, and happier customers.

The impact of Kaizen went beyond Toyota and the car sector. Sony, Honda, and Canon, among other Japanese corporations, embraced such ideas to improve their business practices. The Kaizen technique was further proven, and its reputation as a potent tool for achieving excellence was strengthened by these companies' extensive success in worldwide marketplaces.

Kaizen gained widespread prominence during a pivotal phase in the 1980s. Western corporations started recognizing the strategies that had helped Japanese companies succeed as they increased their global market share and importance. During this time, Japan saw a surge in Western academics and managers interested in studying its management practices. Books such as Masaaki Imai's 1986 publication, "Kaizen: The Key to Japan's Competitive Success," were essential in popularizing Kaizen and emphasizing its capacity to revolutionize corporate operations.

Kaizen's fundamental ideas are rooted in Japanese cultural values like excellence, teamwork, and respect for others. Japanese corporate culture places a high value on teamwork and mutual assistance. The notion that everyone can make improvements, regardless of status, is supported by this cultural basis. Kaizen encourages workers to take pride in their jobs and strive for constant improvement by fostering a sense of ownership and responsibility.

Furthermore, Kaizen is consistent with the Japanese notion of "monozukuri," which means "the art of making things." A strong regard for fine craftsmanship, meticulous attention to detail, and an unwavering quest for perfection are all embodied in monozukuri. The importance of accuracy and quality in Japanese industrial processes is a clear example of this cultural attitude. With its emphasis on problem-solving and minor improvements, Kaizen enhances the monozukuri mindset and aids businesses in meeting strict quality and productivity requirements.

Beyond its use in industry, Kaizen has impacted many facets of Japanese culture. For instance, Japanese clinics and hospitals have implemented Kaizen concepts to enhance patient care, lower errors, and expedite administrative procedures. Better patient outcomes and more economical resource use have resulted from the healthcare industry's emphasis on continual improvement. Similarly, Kaizen ideas have been implemented in education, where academic institutions use them to improve student involvement, administrative procedures, and instructional strategies.

Kaizen has become widely accepted worldwide, adapted, and integrated into many cultural contexts. Although the fundamental ideas are still the same, businesses worldwide have modified Kaizen to meet their particular requirements and difficulties. For example, "Lean" originated in the United States as a variation of the Kaizen principles, emphasizing value maximization through waste reduction. The broad adoption of lean approaches in a variety of industries, including manufacturing, healthcare, and services, demonstrates the adaptability and allure of Kaizen.

In summary, the origins of Kaizen in Japanese society and its history demonstrate a pervasive dedication to ongoing development that has had a significant impact on contemporary management techniques. Kaizen, rooted in the Japanese culture's emphasis on discipline, slow pace, and attention to detail, was codified and made famous in the post-World War II era by introducing quality control techniques and the innovative work of businesses such as Toyota. Since Kaizen principles have extended throughout the world and proven effective in various settings, they have become a mainstay of modern management techniques. By comprehending its cultural and historical roots, we may recognize Kaizen's enduring relevance and revolutionary potential in promoting excellence and continuous improvement.

Key Principles and Values

Kaizen, which translates from Japanese to mean "continuous improvement," is a concept that always emphasizes improving people, processes, and products. Deeply ingrained in Japanese society, the ideas and ideals of Kaizen have crossed national and cultural boundaries to become essential components of effective management strategies all across the world. Understanding these fundamental ideas and ideals is necessary to comprehend how Kaizen promotes organizational and individual development.

The emphasis on gradual rather than drastic improvements is one of the core tenets of Kaizen. This strategy is based on the idea that gradual, tiny adjustments can significantly impact over time. Organizations can make steady progress and prevent the disruptions that often precede large-scale reforms by routinely making little modifications and revisions. These principal highlights that in the quest for excellence, it is crucial to have patience, tenacity, and a long-term perspective.

Consistency is essential because it is strongly related to gradual improvement. Consistency in the context of Kaizen refers to the ongoing, consistent effort to improve procedures and methods. It entails creating a disciplined work environment where ongoing development is ingrained in everyday tasks. This consistency contributes to establishing a steady and predictable environment that makes it possible to methodically identify, apply, and assess improvements. Organizations can lay a solid basis for long-term growth and innovation by promoting consistency.

The importance placed on employee empowerment and involvement is another fundamental tenet of Kaizen. Kaizen acknowledges that workers at all levels have insightful opinions and ideas that can support improvement efforts. Organizations may access knowledge and creativity by promoting employee participation in problem identification and solution suggestions. Employees who follow this principle feel more accountable and have a sense of ownership since they are actively involved in the change process. Employee empowerment fosters teamwork and trust, which makes an organization more adaptable and dynamic.

Employee involvement and the importance of cooperation are closely intertwined. Kaizen encourages problem-solving techniques where people cooperate to accomplish shared objectives. This value stems from the conviction that group efforts produce superior outcomes to solitary pursuits. Organizations may take advantage of different viewpoints and skill sets by encouraging teamwork, which can result in more creative and practical solutions. In addition, teamwork fosters a sense of belonging and mutual support, which are critical for sustaining motivation and a dedication to ongoing development.

Another pillar of Kaizen is the idea of uniform work. Recording and continuously implementing best practices and procedures is known as "standardized work." Ensuring that procedures are followed consistently and predictably lowers errors and variability in the process. Additionally, standardized work offers a reference point for gauging and assessing advancements. Organizations may develop a more dependable and efficient operation and set the stage for future improvements by defining clear standards and norms.

Kaizen also highlights how crucial visual management is. Using visual tools and indicators to convey information quickly is known as visual management. This idea aids in the transparency and understandability of procedures, making it simple for staff members to see irregularities and potential development areas. Decision-making is aided by visual management tools like dashboards, graphs, and charts, which offer immediate feedback. Organizations can improve awareness, accountability, and responsiveness by increasing the visibility and accessibility of information.

The foundation of Kaizen is the idea of eliminating waste, or "muda," as it is known in Japanese. Any resource or activity that does not provide value for the client is considered waste. Overproduction, waiting, transportation, excess inventory, overprocessing, flaws, and underutilized talent are the seven categories of waste that Kaizen identifies. Organizations may enhance quality, cut costs, and streamline operations by identifying and removing waste methodically. This principle promotes the pursuit of efficiency and value and a critical analysis of current procedures.

Root cause analysis is also essential to Kaizen. According to this theory, solving problems' root causes is preferable to treating their symptoms. Methods like cause-and-effect diagrams and the "5 Whys" are frequently employed to probe more into issues and identify their underlying causes. Organizations can develop more durable and practical solutions by concentrating on the underlying cause. Root cause analysis promotes a culture of problem-solving and ongoing education, where errors are seen as chances for development.

Kaizen is based on the continuous learning premise. Continuous learning requires new knowledge and abilities to adjust to changing conditions and enhance performance. Kaizen promotes an open-minded, curious mindset where people always look for ways to improve their abilities. This idea fosters creativity and flexibility in society and aids in professional and personal growth. Organizations that practice continuous learning can also better meet market needs and maintain competitiveness.

Respect for individuals is one of the core principles of Kaizen. This principle emphasizes how crucial treating workers respectfully and recognizing their contributions is. People in a kaizen atmosphere are respected, cherished, and encouraged. Respect for people entails offering chances for development, paying attention to the opinions and worries of staff members, and establishing a welcoming and safe work environment. Companies may create a solid, driven team dedicated to ongoing development by appreciating and respecting their employees.

Lastly, the foundation of Kaizen is the idea of customer attention. This idea highlights how crucial it is to comprehend and satisfy the requirements and expectations of your customers. Kaizen pushes businesses to always look for methods to improve customer satisfaction and to see quality from the customer's point of view. Organizations may create goods and services that provide more value and develop enduring relationships by prioritizing consumer needs. A customer-focused approach propels innovation and excellence as businesses endeavor to surpass client expectations and maintain a competitive edge.

To sum up, the fundamental ideas and ideals of Kaizen offer a thorough framework for attaining ongoing development in both individual and group settings. A culture of excellence and innovation is created by combining these principles: gradual improvement, consistency, teamwork, respect for people, root cause analysis, visual management, waste elimination, continuous learning, and customer focus. By adopting these ideas and values, individuals and organizations can create a dynamic and adaptable atmosphere that promotes long-term success and growth. Kaizen's capacity to drive significant, long-lasting changes and adapt to various circumstances makes it relevant today.

The Kaizen Approach vs. Traditional Improvement Methods

In stark contrast to conventional improvement techniques, the Kaizen approach provides a unique methodology for improvement. Translating to "continuous improvement," Kaizen is a Japanese concept that prioritizes tiny, gradual improvements over significant, drastic ones. This strategy substantially affects how people and organizations strive for quality, efficiency, and growth.

The aim and scope of Kaizen and traditional improvement techniques are among their most notable distinctions. Conventional approaches frequently place a higher priority on radical, significant changes meant to produce noticeable outcomes quickly. These approaches are usually implemented in response to urgent issues or opportunities and may entail substantial overhauls of systems, processes, or organizations. The Kaizen approach, on the other hand, is more concerned with making small, ongoing changes. It aims to gradually improve current procedures by making several tiny, doable adjustments that add substantial long-term advantages. This way of thinking is based on the idea that gradual advancement over time is safer and more sustainable than sudden, significant shifts.

According to the Kaizen approach, all staff members, from upper management to frontline workers, should be included in the improvement process. Change projects under traditional improvement techniques are frequently spearheaded by external consultants or senior leadership, with minimal involvement from those directly involved in day-to-day operations. This top-down strategy can result in employee resistance and lack of buy-in because they may believe their experiences and insights should be more appreciated. Conversely, Kaizen promotes a collaborative and participatory culture. It encourages staff members of all levels to point out inefficiencies and provide recommendations for enhancements by utilizing their unique knowledge and viewpoints. This bottom-up strategy increases the likelihood of effective implementation by creating a sense of ownership and commitment among employees and producing a wealth of improvement ideas.

The emphasis Kaizen places on waste reduction is another critical differentiator. Conventional approaches to improvement frequently focus on reaching performance goals or raising productivity. Although these objectives are significant, they may result in waste and inefficiency if they are not appropriately handled. Kaizen emphasizes locating and eliminating waste (called "muda" in Japanese), which can take many forms. Some examples of waste include excess inventory, waiting periods, overproduction, needless transportation, and flaws. Kaizen assists businesses in streamlining their operations, cutting expenses, and raising quality, resulting in more effective and efficient processes. It does this by methodically eliminating waste.

Kaizen is primarily implemented through straightforward, valuable tools and methods easily understood and used by staff members at all levels. A planned and systematic approach to facilitating continuous improvement is provided by these tools, which include the Plan-Do-Check-Act (PDCA) cycle, the 5S method (Sort, Set in order, Shine, Standardize, Sustain), and the usage of visual management. On the other hand, traditional improvement methods could entail intricate structures and procedures that need particular expertise and training to be implemented successfully. This intricacy may limit the possibility for broad improvement and erect obstacles to acceptance.

The Kaizen strategy is distinct in that it places a greater focus on sustainability and long-term planning. Conventional improvement techniques are frequently motivated to satisfy quarterly performance targets or react quickly to competition challenges. Although these approaches can yield quick results, they can also have unforeseen effects, such as raising employee stress levels, lowering quality, or emphasizing band-aids rather than long-term cures. But Kaizen puts sustainability and long-term success first. It pushes businesses to look beyond short-term benefits and evaluate how their decisions will affect overall performance in the long run. Kaizen helps organizations develop resilience and adaptability to prosper in a fast-paced, cutthroat market by promoting a culture of continuous improvement.

Furthermore, the Kaizen methodology heavily emphasizes measurement and data's role in promoting change. Conventional approaches may use partial knowledge, anecdotal evidence, or intuition to inform decisions. This may result in less-than-ideal results and lost chances for advancement. On the other hand, Kaizen promotes a data-driven strategy in which choices are made in light of precise and pertinent facts. Process mapping, performance measurements, and root cause analysis are tools used to map out areas for improvement, track developments, and assess the success of modifications. By emphasizing data strongly, it is possible to monitor and validate results and ensure that efforts to improve are supported by impartial evidence.

The Kaizen approach's capacity to alter corporate culture is among its most significant effects. Conventional improvement techniques are frequently perceived as project- or episodic, resulting in a recurring pattern of change initiatives interspersed with intervals of relative stability. Employees may feel unsettled and disturbed, and they may believe that continuous improvement is more of an infrequent than an occasional endeavor. However, Kaizen incorporates the idea of continual improvement into an organization's regular procedures and processes. It fosters a culture where workers continuously seek methods to improve operations, view setbacks as chances for improvement, and value and reward creativity and innovation. The way an organization functions and workers think and act can undergo significant and long-lasting changes due to this cultural shift.

To sum up, the Kaizen approach to improvement presents a unique and remarkably successful substitute for conventional methods. Kaizen is a methodology that promotes continuous improvement and can result in significant and long-lasting benefits. It does this by emphasizing small, incremental changes, involving all employees in the improvement process, emphasizing waste reduction, using straightforward and valuable tools, prioritizing long-term sustainability, and depending on data-driven decision-making. This strategy develops a more engaged and motivated staff and improves operational efficiency and quality, eventually increasing organizational resilience and success. The fundamental principles and practices of Kaizen provide a valuable foundation for attaining excellence and sustained growth as firms attempt to navigate an increasingly competitive and complicated landscape.

CHAPTER II

The Psychology Behind Continuous Improvement

The Role of Mindset in Personal Growth

A person's attitude significantly impacts their ability to grow personally since it shapes their self-perception, sense of competence, and future possibilities. A person's mentality, commonly described as a collection of attitudes and beliefs that influence their behavior and perspective on life, is a significant factor in determining whether they face issues with a growth-oriented, resilient, and resilient mindset or a fixed, avoidant, resigned mindset. The importance of mentality in personal development will be discussed in this section, along with how it affects behavior, shapes results, and ultimately defines a person's potential for success, learning, and development.

The differentiation between the two main mindsets—the growth mindset and the fixed mindset—lays the foundation of mindset theory. Those who embrace a growth mindset are empowered by the belief that they can improve their intelligence and skills through hard work, practice, and study. They view obstacles as stepping stones to improvement, understand that failure is a necessary part of the learning journey, and persist in the face of challenges. In contrast, individuals with a fixed mindset perceive IQ and skill levels as unchangeable traits. They avoid tasks for fear of failure, interpret failure as a reflection of their inherent limitations, and give up easily when faced with difficulty.

Psychology research has demonstrated the significant influence that mindset can have on various elements of personal development and growth. Studies show that individuals with a growth mindset are more likely to actively seek opportunities for personal growth, embrace challenges, and persevere in the face of adversity. They also tend to set high goals, employ effective study techniques, and achieve success in their endeavors. Conversely, those with a fixed mindset are more inclined to avoid challenges, give up quickly when things don't go their way, and exhibit lower levels of motivation and self-esteem.

Furthermore, a person's perspective might affect how they react to criticism and comments. People with a growth mentality regard criticism and comments as beneficial chances for growth and development. They look for chances for improvement, value constructive criticism, and use it to pinpoint areas that still need work. On the other hand, people who have a fixed perspective could see criticism and comments as personal jabs or dangers to their self-worth. They could become defensive or unreceptive to criticism, brushing it off or failing to see it as a chance for improvement.

Additionally, a person's perspective might influence how they react to failure and setbacks. People with a growth mindset see failure as a chance for personal progress and a normal part of the learning process. They learn from their mistakes, get back up fast after failing, and turn setbacks into opportunities for growth. On the other hand, those with a fixed mindset could see a lack of success as proof of their innate shortcomings. Failure may demoralize or dishearten them, causing them to give up on their objectives or shy away from future difficulties to preserve their self-esteem.

Moreover, a person's resilience and ability to cope with stress and adversity can be influenced by their mindset. Research suggests that individuals with a growth mindset are more resilient, bouncing back more effectively from obstacles and disappointments. They maintain a positive outlook on life, handling stress more effectively. In contrast, those with a fixed mindset may struggle to cope with stress and adversity, leading to increased levels of anxiety, despair, and other negative emotions.

Furthermore, a person's thinking might affect their social interactions and relationships. People with a growth mentality are more likely to be cooperative, understanding, and open-minded in their interpersonal interactions. They seek out different viewpoints, value other people's opinions, and are open to gaining knowledge from their experiences. On the other hand, people who have a fixed worldview could be more exclusive, protective, and aggressive in their interpersonal interactions. People could find it difficult to take criticism or comments from others because they perceive it as a danger to their status or sense of self.

To sum up, mindset plays a significant and diverse role in personal development, impacting people's attitudes, and actions and results in various spheres of their lives. A person's mindset affects how they view their abilities, capacity for growth, and self. People with a growth attitude rise to difficulties, see failure as a chance to learn, and keep going after obstacles. On the other hand, those with a fixed attitude could shy away from difficulties, give up quickly when faced with barriers, and find it challenging to deal with setbacks and hardship. People can realize their full potential, seize chances for learning and progress, and lead more successful and fulfilling lives by cultivating a growth mindset.

Growth Mindset vs. Fixed Mindset

The concept of mindset, particularly the dichotomy between a growth and a fixed mindset, has gained significant traction in recent times due to its profound impact on learning, achievement, and personal development. These terms, 'growth mindset' and 'fixed mindset ', were first introduced by psychologist Carol Dweck, offering two contrasting perspectives on potential, aptitude, and intellect. In this section, we will delve into the nuances of these mindsets, their influence on behavior, attitudes, and outcomes, and explore strategies for cultivating a growth mindset to unlock one's full potential.

The foundation of the growth mindset is the idea that intelligence, skills, and talents are not permanent attributes but may instead be developed and fostered through work, persistence, and education. People with a growth mindset see obstacles as chances for personal development, accept failure as an inevitable part of learning, and persevere in facing difficulties. They are always looking for ways to learn and grow and are resilient, flexible, and receptive to criticism. On the other hand, those who have a fixed mindset think that skills and intelligence are natural qualities that cannot be enhanced or modified. They shy away from tasks out of fear of failing, see failure as a sign of their innate shortcomings, and give up readily in the face of difficulty.

Empirical studies have demonstrated the crucial role of mentality in molding conduct, perspectives, and consequences in various life domains, such as learning, employment, interpersonal connections, and individual growth. Studies have shown, for instance, that students with a growth mindset are more likely than their peers with a fixed mindset to seek out complex assignments, employ efficient learning techniques, and succeed academically. Employees who with a growth mentality at work are more willing to innovate, take on new tasks, and adjust to change, improving performance and opening up career progression opportunities.

Moreover, an individual's mindset significantly influences their response to feedback. Those with a growth mindset perceive criticism as a valuable opportunity for personal growth. They actively seek ways to improve, value constructive feedback, and use it to enhance their performance. Conversely, individuals with a fixed mindset might interpret criticism as a personal attack or a threat to their self-worth. They may respond defensively, dismissing feedback or failing to recognize it as a chance for self-improvement.

In addition, a person's thinking influences how they view failure and setbacks. People with a growth mindset see failure as a chance for personal progress and a normal part of the learning process. They learn from their mistakes, get back up fast after failing, and turn setbacks into opportunities for growth. On the other hand, those with a fixed mindset could see a lack of success as proof of their innate shortcomings. Failure may demoralize or dishearten them, causing them to give up on their objectives or shy away from future difficulties to preserve their self-esteem.

In addition, a person's resilience and capacity to handle stress and hardship are influenced by their thinking. According to research, those with a growth mentality are more able to bounce back from obstacles and disappointments. They are more resilient to hardship, have a more upbeat attitude, and can handle stress better. Individuals who possess a fixed mindset, on the other hand, could find it challenging to manage stress and hardship, leading to increased levels of worry, despair, and other negative feelings.

Furthermore, a person's thinking might affect their social interactions and relationships. People with a growth mentality are more likely to be cooperative, understanding, and open-minded in their interpersonal interactions. They seek out different viewpoints, value other people's opinions, and are open to gaining knowledge from their experiences. On the other hand, people who have a fixed worldview could be more exclusive, protective, and aggressive in their interpersonal interactions. People could find it difficult to take criticism or comments from others because they perceive it as a danger to their status or sense of self.

To sum up, the differentiation between a growth mindset and a fixed mindset holds significant consequences for individual progress, education, and accomplishment. People with a growth attitude rise to difficulties, see failure as a chance to learn, and keep going after obstacles. They are always looking for ways to learn and grow and are resilient, flexible, and receptive to criticism. On the other hand, those with a fixed attitude could shy away from difficulties, give up quickly when faced with barriers, and find it challenging to deal with setbacks and hardship. People can realize their full potential, seize chances for growth and learning, and lead more successful and fulfilling lives by adopting a growth mindset.

How Kaizen Promotes a Growth Mindset

As Kaizen, the Japanese philosophy of continuous improvement stands out as a potent catalyst for fostering growth in individuals and businesses. What sets Kaizen apart is its unwavering commitment to excellence and continual improvement through small, gradual changes to systems, processes, and Kaizen. This unique approach promotes a culture of continuous improvement and progress and instills in individuals and organizations the ability to embrace obstacles and failure as a valuable learning opportunity. This section will delve into the unique aspects of Kaizen that to foster a growth mindset, exploring its guiding concepts, methods, and applications in advancing individual and group development.

Kaizen's emphasis on continual improvement is one of the main ways it fosters a growth attitude. Kaizen acknowledges that continuous learning, adaptability, and invention are necessary for improvement, which is a never-ending process. Through every day small-scale system and process modifications, people and organizations may accelerate development, maximize efficiency, and produce long-term, sustainable outcomes. People are encouraged to embrace a mindset that values growth, views obstacles as chances for learning, and accepts change as a necessary component of the path toward greatness by this emphasis on continuous improvement.

Furthermore, it encourages people to actively seek improvement opportunities and take ownership of their development, which supports a growth mentality. In contrast to traditional improvement techniques, which initiatives or instructions from above could influence, Kaizen gives people at all organizational levels the authority to see issues, make recommendations for improvements, and implement those suggestions. Employee empowerment is promoted by Kaizen, which involves employees in improvement initiatives and gives them a say in decision-making procedures. This motivates people to pursue growth chances on their initiative, take a proactive approach to their development, and always strive for perfection.

Furthermore, it encourages a growth mentality by redefining failure as an inevitable and necessary learning component. The Kaizen philosophy views failure as a chance for introspection, growth, and learning rather than reflecting a person's intrinsic shortcomings or incapacity. Kaizen fosters resiliency, endurance, and a positive outlook on problems by encouraging people to see failure as a stepping stone to success rather than a barrier. This promotes the creation of a growth mentality in people, which appreciates the effort, views setbacks as transient, and keeps an eye on long-term improvement.

Furthermore, it supports a growth mindset by encouraging a culture of experimentation, creativity, and invention. To improve, Kaizen pushes people to try out novel concepts, try various strategies, and take measured risks. Providing a secure and encouraging atmosphere conducive to ingenuity and inventiveness enables people to think beyond conventional thinking, question established norms, and expand possibilities. This promotes a way of thinking that prioritizes discovery, accepts and views failure as a necessary outcome of creativity and experimentation.

Furthermore, it encourages growth by highlighting the significance of introspection and feedback in the learning process. Kaizen encourages people to ask for and consider input from others to reflect on their experiences and use that feedback to identify areas where they may improve. Through facilitating contemplation and self-evaluation, Kaizen assists people in gaining a more profound comprehension of their advantages, disadvantages, and potential growth areas. This promotes the adoption of a growth mindset in people, wherein they appreciate feedback, view it as an invaluable source of knowledge, and utilize it to further their personal and professional development.

Additionally, it encourages a growth attitude by giving people the instruments, materials, and assistance they require for success. Kaizen strongly emphasizes the value of education, training, and skill development in fostering excellence and kaizens. Investing in people's development and giving them chances to learn and grow enables them to realize their full potential and accomplish their objectives. This promotes a growth attitude in people who value education, view obstacles as chances for personal improvement, and have faith in one's ability to achieve through hard work and persistence.

To sum up, Kaizen is an effective catalyst for encouraging growth in individuals and organizations. Through its emphasis on friendship, resilience, experimentation, feedback, and support along with continuous improvement, Kaizen pushes people to adopt a mindset that values progress, welcomes difficulties and views failure as an inevitable part of learning. In today's fast-paced and constantly evolving environment, this aids people in acquiring the attitudes, behaviors, and beliefs necessary for personal and organizational success.

CHAPTER III

The Kaizen Cycle

The PDCA (Plan-Do-Check-Act) Cycle

Organizations worldwide have embraced the PDCA (Plan-Do-Check-Act) cycle, also called the Deming cycle or the Shewhart cycle, as a potent framework for problem-solving and continuous development. The PDCA cycle, created by renowned statistician Walter A. Shewhart in the 1920s and made famous by quality management expert W. Edwards Deming, offers a systematic way to improve products, services, and processes systematically.

The Plan phase of the PDCA cycle is when goals and objectives are defined, and a strategy for achieving them is created. In this stage, companies pinpoint areas needing development, establish clear goals, and develop plans and methods to reach them. This may entail carrying out research, obtaining information, and interacting with stakeholders to ensure the strategy is informed and in line with corporate priorities and objectives. By offering a schedule for execution and assessment, the Plan phase of the PDCA cycle establishes the groundwork for the later stages.

The Do phase of the PDCA cycle is when the plan is carried out, and improvement initiatives are carried out in compliance with the predetermined plan. In this stage, companies implement their strategies by distributing funds, designating roles, and carrying out the assigned tasks for improvement. To support the improvement initiatives this may entail educating staff members, putting new policies or procedures into place, and altering infrastructure or systems. During the implementation stage, companies start to witness concrete outcomes from their enhancement campaigns.

Check is the third stage of the PDCA cycle, during which goals and objectives are assessed to see if they have been met. Progress is tracked. Organizations gather and examine data during this phase to evaluate the success of the improvement projects and spot any plan deviations. Determining areas for improvement and assessing stakeholder satisfaction may entail performing audits or inspections, comparing actual performance to set targets, and requesting stakeholder feedback. The Check phase helps decision-making for subsequent PDCA cycle iterations and offers insightful information about how well the improvement efforts work.

In order to further enhance performance and accomplish the intended goals, modifications are made in the fourth and final phase of the PDCA cycle, Act, based on the findings of the Check phase. Organizations address any problems or shortcomings found during the Check phase by taking remedial action during this phase and making any required changes to the plan. To fill in the gaps and seize chances for even more improvement, this can entail adjusting goals, honing tactics, and putting new improvement projects into action. The Act phase ensures that businesses continuously learn, adapt, and progress in their quest for excellence by closing the loop on the PDCA cycle. This emphasis on continuous learning and improvement is a key aspect of the PDCA cycle, highlighting the importance of ongoing development and the potential for businesses to always strive for excellence.

One of its main advantages is the PDCA cycle's cyclical nature, which allows businesses to continually cycle through the phases of Plan, Do, Check, and Act to promote continuous innovation and development. Organizations can systematically find areas for improvement, put practical solutions in place, and track outcomes to ensure goals are met by adhering to the PDCA cycle. Iterative approaches help firms stay ahead of the competition by fostering a culture of continuous development and enabling them to respond to emerging issues and changing situations.

In addition, the PDCA cycle offers an organized framework for problem-solving that is applicable to many different businesses and situations. The PDCA cycle provides a versatile and adaptive method for attaining quantifiable outcomes, regardless of the organization's goals: better customer service, higher-quality products, or more efficient corporate procedures. This adaptability of the PDCA cycle empowers businesses, giving them the confidence that they can effectively tackle any issue and foster enduring improvements, no matter the complexity or nature of the problem.

In conclusion, businesses looking to attain excellence and spur innovation have adopted the PDCA (Plan-Do-Check-Act) cycle as a potent framework for problem-solving and continuous development. Organizations can methodically identify areas for improvement, implement workable solutions, and evaluate outcomes to ensure goals are met by adhering to the iterative Plan, Do, Check, and Act process. The PDCA cycle promotes a culture of continuous improvement, which also helps firms adjust to changing circumstances and gives teams the tools they need to continuously innovate and achieve excellence in all facets of their business operations.

Breaking Down the Cycle Step-by-Step

Stepwise deconstruction of the improvement cycle is crucial to comprehending and successfully using continuous improvement concepts represented in techniques such as Kaizen. The cycle, also known as the Plan-Do-Check-Act (PDCA) cycle, offers an organized structure for determining issues, testing fixes, and fostering gradual advancements over time. Every cycle stage, from preparation and execution to assessment and modification, is vital to the improvement process. In this section, we shall dissect the PDCA cycle in detail, going over its elements, guiding principles, and uses in promoting organizational excellence and continuous development.

Preparation is the first phase in the PDCA cycle, and it entails setting goals, recognizing issues, and creating improvement methods. In this stage, people work in groups or individually to assess the situation as it is, establish clear objectives or aims for development, and create plans of action to reach these goals. Another aspect of planning is making backup plans to deal with potential roadblocks or impediments to accomplishment. Organizations can focus their resources, coordinate their efforts, and ensure everyone works toward the same goal by establishing clear goals and objectives upfront.

The proposed changes are implemented during the implementation phase, which follows the establishment of the plan. This step entails carrying out the action plan, assembling resources, and coordinating efforts to put the suggested changes into practice. Testing new systems, methods, or processes on a small scale may be necessary to evaluate their efficacy and spot any possible problems or difficulties during implementation. All pertinent stakeholders must be included in the implementation process to ensure everyone is on board with and committed to the suggested changes. Through proactive employee involvement in the implementation process, firms can leverage their knowledge, perspectives, and inventiveness to facilitate significant advancements.

The next stage after implementation is to verify or assess the outcomes of the changes that were put into place. This stage entails gathering information, monitoring performance, and evaluating how improvements affect important metrics or goals. Some examples of evaluation techniques are comparing actual results to anticipated outcomes, performing root cause analysis to pinpoint the variables influencing performance, and getting stakeholder input to understand their perspectives and experiences. Organizations can ascertain whether the suggested improvements have produced the expected effects and pinpoint any areas that require additional development or adjustment by carefully analyzing the consequences of the changes that have been implemented.

The last phase in the PDCA cycle involves acting or modifying the plan in light of the evaluation's findings and lessons learned. Based on the evaluation's findings, decisions must be made at this phase regarding whether to keep the established improvements in place, modify them, or scrap them entirely. Organizations may standardize the new processes, procedures, or systems and incorporate them into their operations if the enhancements have produced the desired results. Organizations may need to review the action plan, find alternate solutions, and create a new strategy to address the underlying problems if the improvements have yet to produce the expected results. Organizations can promote continual development and produce long-lasting gains by iterating and improving the improvement process frequently in response to input and outcomes.

It is crucial to remember that the PDCA cycle is an ongoing, iterative process rather than a single, one-time occurrence. Organizations can start the cycle again after the first one is over, incorporating the knowledge from the first cycle to guide their subsequent changes. Organizations can reach ever-higher levels of performance and quality, drive continuous improvement, and adapt to changing conditions by repeatedly repeating the PDCA cycle.

Furthermore, an organization's procedures, departments, and overall structure can all benefit from applying the PDCA cycle. The PDCA cycle's four guiding principles—plan, do, check, and act—remain the same regardless of the size or scope of the improvement project. Organizations can build a culture of continuous improvement, empower people to drive positive change, and accomplish their strategic objectives more effectively and efficiently by systematically and consistently implementing the PDCA cycle.

To sum up, comprehending and successfully applying continuous improvement concepts requires dissecting the development cycle step-by-step. A systematic framework for recognizing issues, trying out fixes, and achieving gradual advancements over time is offered by the PDCA cycle. Organizations may drive continuous improvement, adapt to changing situations, and attain ever-higher levels of performance and excellence by adhering to the four steps of the PDCA cycle: plan, do, check, and act. In today's dynamic and competitive business climate, businesses can achieve their strategic objectives more effectively and efficiently by empowering workers to drive positive change and developing a culture of continuous improvement.

Practical Examples of the Kaizen Cycle in Action

The Plan-Do-Check-Act (PDCA) cycle, commonly called the Kaizen cycle, is an essential component of the Kaizen approach to continuous development. This iteration represents a systematic approach to executing, overseeing, and enhancing enhancements. Examining real-world instances of the Kaizen cycle's implementation in various settings and industries will help you appreciate the cycle's strength and adaptability. These instances show how the Kaizen cycle may improve productivity, quality, and efficiency while bringing about significant change.

The production process at Toyota is a prominent illustration of the Kaizen cycle in action. Toyota's success and reputation for quality can largely be attributed to its application of Kaizen principles. The PDCA cycle is employed in Toyota's production system to enhance assembly line operations continuously. For example, when a problem occurs with a specific process, like a bottleneck in the manufacturing line, Toyota workers are urged to participate in the Plan phase by recognizing the issue and suggesting possible fixes. A small-scale test of the proposed solution is implemented during the Do phase. During the Check phase, data on the test's efficacy is gathered through observation. Ultimately, the Act phase sees the revision or elimination of poor solutions while the standardization and implementation of effective ones throughout the manufacturing line. Toyota can continuously improve its operations while upholding high efficiency and quality standards because of this iterative process.

Healthcare, especially in hospital settings, is another industry where the Kaizen cycle is put to use. Ensuring patient safety, boosting operational efficiency, and improving care quality are complicated problems for hospitals. Hospitals can systematically address these difficulties by implementing the Kaizen cycle. For example, the PDCA cycle can be used by a hospital to shorten emergency room wait times for patients. Staff members would examine waiting times at the moment and pinpoint delays caused during the Plan phase. They could suggest improvements to patient flow management, streamlined triage processes, or resource reallocation. These solutions would be tested in a limited setting during the Do phase. To ascertain how the adjustments will affect wait times, data collection and analysis will be conducted during the Check phase. Ultimately, effective modifications would be implemented more widely during the Act phase, while ineffective tactics would be reassessed and modified. This continual improvement method can significantly improve operational effectiveness and patient care.

The Kaizen cycle is also quite effective in the retail sector, where customer satisfaction and operational effectiveness are crucial. Take the example of a retail chain that wants to enhance its overstock and stockout procedures. To find inefficiencies and opportunities for improvement, the business would examine its present inventory levels, sales information, and supply chain procedures during the Plan phase. Some possible remedies are using sophisticated inventory management software, improving supplier connections, or putting in place a just-in-time inventory system. These solutions would be evaluated in a few stores during the Do phase. To assess the effects of the modifications, the Check phase would involve keeping an eye on inventory levels, sales results, and customer comments. Ultimately, the Act phase would see the implementation of successful techniques throughout all stores, along with the refinement or replacement of poor ones. With this iterative approach, the retail chain can save expenses, increase customer satisfaction, and maintain ideal inventory levels.

The Kaizen cycle can be applied in the education sector to improve student results and instructional strategies. The PDCA cycle is a tool that schools can use to address low student performance in a given subject. Teachers and administrators would examine student performance data during the Plan phase to pinpoint the precise areas pupils struggle with. They could suggest treatments, including curriculum modifications, resource additions, or innovative teaching methods. These interventions would be tested in small classrooms during the Do phase. Data on student performance and engagement would be gathered during the Check phase to assess the interventions' success. Ultimately, the Act phase would see the expansion of successful interventions into additional classrooms and the revision or replacement of less successful ones. Schools may better meet the requirements of their students and enhance educational achievements by customizing their teaching strategies with this continuous improvement approach.

The software development business can benefit from the Kaizen cycle, where quick iterations and ongoing improvement are essential. The PDCA cycle is a tool that software development teams can use to increase the effectiveness of their process. During the Plan phase, the team would find inefficiencies and bottlenecks in their existing workflow, including protracted review periods or a high frequency of code errors. They could suggest fixes like introducing automated testing, applying agile approaches, or improving code review procedures. These solutions would be tested throughout several development cycles in the Do phase. To evaluate the effects of the changes, metrics, including development speed, bug frequency, and code quality, would be analyzed during the Check phase. Ultimately, the Act phase would see the adoption of successful solutions as standard procedures and the refinement or discarding of less successful ones. The development team may continuously enhance its workflow through this iterative method, which leads to quicker software delivery and better quality.

The Kaizen cycle can be applied in the service sector to boost operational effectiveness and customer service. The PDCA cycle, for instance, may be used by a chain of hotels to raise customer satisfaction. During the Plan phase, the hotel would review reviews from past visitors to find recurring issues or areas that needed attention, such as customer service, cleanliness of the rooms, or check-in procedures. They could suggest fixes like implementing a digital check-in system, improving employee training, or doing more frequent cleanings. These solutions would be tried in a select hotel during the Do phase. Data on staff performance, operational effectiveness, and guest happiness will be gathered and analyzed throughout the Check phase to assess the adjustments' success. Ultimately, the Act phase would see the implementation of successful techniques throughout all hotels, along with the refinement or replacement of poor ones. The hotel chain's ongoing improvement process helps it keep a competitive edge, increase client pleasure, and boost operational effectiveness.

In summary, the PDCA cycle, also known as the Kaizen cycle, is an effective technique for continuous improvement used in various settings and sectors. Companies can achieve small but meaningful, long-term gains by adhering to the systematic planning, doing, checking, and acting process. Empirical instances drawn from the manufacturing, healthcare, retail, education, software development, and service sectors illustrate how the Kaizen cycle can effectively promote significant transformation and augment effectiveness, caliber, and output. The Kaizen cycle offers an organized and practical method for continual improvement, whether for resolving operational inefficiencies, raising customer satisfaction, or improving product quality.

CHAPTER IV

Kaizen at Home

Organizing Your Living Space

Living space organization is more than just cleaning; it's essential to improving your general productivity and well-being. Your quality of life can be significantly enhanced, productivity can rise, and stress can greatly decrease in an orderly environment. Organizing storage, establishing zones for functionality, clearing clutter, and upholding order are all part of the process. Create a peaceful atmosphere that supports your everyday activities and personal objectives by methodically structuring your living area.

Decluttering your living area is the first step towards organizing it. This entails assessing your possessions and choosing what to donate, keep, and eliminate. Clutter results from people collecting things that they no longer need or use over time. A rigorous evaluation of each item's usefulness and sentimental worth is necessary before decluttering. You can clear space and lessen mental and visual clutter by removing stuff you don't need. Although this procedure can be complex, creating a well-organized and valuable living space is necessary. One area at a time, such as a closet, drawer, or room, can make it more manageable. The task becomes less daunting and more doable when divided into smaller parts.

Creating functional zones in your living area is the next step after decluttering. Every space should have a distinct function, whether for working, resting, or cooking. You may better manage your activities and utilize your space by creating clearly defined zones. For instance, you can set aside spaces in the kitchen for storing, preparing, and cooking food. Set aside a space in the living area for socializing, reading, and entertainment. Setting up a specific workspace with all the required equipment and supplies is what a home office would entail. Increase productivity and reduce time wasted looking for things or changing between tasks by setting your living area into functional zones.

Organizing your living space also involves making the most of your storage. You can maintain objects' organization and accessibility with efficient storage options. A range of storage solutions, including shelves, bins, baskets, drawers, and cabinets, should be used. Because it makes the most of the available height, vertical storage can be beneficial in limited spaces. Furthermore, you can tailor your storage with modular solutions to meet your unique requirements and space limitations. Maintaining order and rapidly identifying the contents of storage containers can be facilitated by labeling them. To ensure your storage options continue to suit your needs as your belongings and way of life evolve, it's critical to assess and update them periodically.

It takes regularity and constant work to keep your living area organized. Create daily and weekly routines to maintain your space's organization once you've finished. A few examples are making your bed every morning, returning goods to their proper locations after usage, and scheduling a brief tidy-up period each week. Getting into the habit of developing these behaviors can help you keep your surroundings tidy and orderly and stop clutter from building up. To further guarantee that everyone helps preserve order, include all home members in the organizing process and assign shared duties.

Making your living space a reflection of your style and a place that promotes your well-being is essential to organizing it. You should feel motivated and at ease in your living environment. Include artwork, plants, and ornamental accents that make you happy and express your individuality. Pay close attention to the lighting, color schemes, and furniture placement for a pleasant and welcoming ambiance. A well-designed and arranged environment can benefit your attitude, energy levels, and general quality of life.

A digital organization should be taken into account in your living area in addition to physical organization. Many people's possessions of digital files, cords, and electronic devices add to the mess and disarray. Putting digital organizing methods into practice can enhance the physical organization of your area. To keep cords and chargers organized, you can designate a specific charging station for your devices, use cable management software, and routinely tidy up your desktop and digital files. Keeping your digital area organized will increase productivity and decrease distractions.

Optimizing the flow and arrangement of your house is another aspect of organizing your living area. Think about how you use your location and arrange furniture and other items to make it easier to move around and get to. For instance, ensure that furniture is arranged to produce a logical and practical flow and that all pathways are clear. Sort objects in the kitchen according to how often you use them and how close they are to chores that require them. Arrange the bed and storage items in the bedroom so that the space feels peaceful and comfortable. Your room may be more valuable and pleasurable with careful arrangement and movement.

You can help the environment and your house by organizing with sustainability. When decluttering, instead of throwing away stuff, think about recycling or giving them. Repurpose or upcycle objects when possible, and opt for sustainable storage alternatives. As a bonus, consider forming practices like utilizing reusable containers, cutting out single-use items, and installing energy-efficient lighting that lower waste and energy usage. A healthier and more environmentally friendly home can be achieved by planning your living area with sustainability.

There are substantial psychological advantages to structuring your living area. Untidy and disorderly surroundings can exacerbate tension, worry, and overload. A neat and ordered environment, on the other hand, might encourage feelings of peace, control, and well-being. Organizing oneself can be a therapeutic activity that brings clarity and a sense of success. You may improve your general quality of life by designing an environment promoting mental and emotional well-being.

Your productivity and attentiveness can both be enhanced by organizing your living area. Your ability to focus on activities is improved, and distractions are decreased in a clutter-free environment. You can save time and feel less frustrated when everything is readily available and has a designated spot. For the places where you study or work, this is especially crucial. For example, having a tidy home office can increase your productivity and creativity, which will help you reach your objectives more successfully.

To sum up, arranging your living area is a complex process that includes preserving order, maximizing storage, decluttering, and creating valuable zones. By methodically taking care of these factors, you may establish a productive and pleasant atmosphere that improves your well-being and quality of life. Your style is reflected in a well-organized area that facilitates your use of control and tranquility.

Your physical and emotional wellbeing will significantly benefit from the time and energy you put into organizing your living space, whether that organizing is through furniture moving, decluttering, or finding the best storage solutions. A room that is well arranged represents your style, facilitates day-to-day tasks, and inspires control and serenity. Making your living environment more organized will have a significant impact on your physical and mental well-being, whether you're decluttering, moving furniture, or finding the best storage options.

Improving Daily Routines

One of the most effective ways to boost productivity, efficiency, and general well-being is to improve daily routines. Daily routines are the habits, duties, and pursuits that organize our days and impact our pleasure and prosperity. By making the most out of these routines, we may prioritize our objectives, better manage our time, and develop wholesome habits that lead to happy, satisfying lives. Numerous methods for enhancing everyday routines can result in beneficial adjustments in various areas of our lives.

First, the morning ritual creates the atmosphere for the entire day. An effective morning ritual can improve mood, focus, and productivity. It can also raise energy levels. Engaging in daily routines that enhance mental and physical health, like working out, practicing meditation, or keeping a journal, is crucial. By lowering stress, boosting resilience, and improving mental clarity, these exercises can prepare you for a successful and rewarding day. Furthermore, implementing wholesome routines like drinking water, having a balanced breakfast, and getting enough sleep will enhance general vitality and well-being.

Setting objectives and establishing priorities for chores is a crucial part of enhancing everyday routines. Achieving targeted results and optimizing productivity need proficient time management. By setting and achieving these goals, we can focus our energies on projects that are consistent with our values and ambitions. This could entail making to-do lists, planning out chores, and dividing more ambitious objectives into smaller, more doable ones. We may better utilize our time, decrease procrastination, and move closer to our long-term goals by practicing proactive time management.

It's critical to include frequent breaks and leisure into our daily routines in addition to goal-setting. We may refuel, relax, and revitalize ourselves by pausing, which is crucial for preserving our focus, creativity, and general well-being. Walking, stretching, or taking up a hobby helps lower stress, avoid burnout, and enhance mental and emotional resilience. We may improve our general quality of life and sustainably control our energy and productivity levels throughout the day by balancing work and play.

Additionally, practicing presence and mindfulness in our daily lives can significantly impact our mental and emotional well-being. Being mindful entails observing the here and now with acceptance, curiosity, and openness. We may lower stress, raise self-awareness, and enhance emotional regulation by implementing mindfulness techniques like meditation, deep breathing, and mindful eating into our everyday routines. Additionally, mindfulness can improve our resilience and general well-being by helping us make deliberate decisions, stay focused, and deal with life's obstacles.

Enhancing everyday routines also entails making our workspaces and physical surroundings as productive and focused as possible. A neat and uncluttered workstation can boost creativity, decrease distractions, and increase focus. We may create an environment that encourages productivity and creativity by clearing out physical clutter, arranging equipment and supplies, and reducing outside distractions. Furthermore, adding features like plants, natural light, and ergonomic furniture can improve well-being and productivity even more in the workplace.

Moreover, keeping balance and avoiding burnout depend on us making self-care and well-being a priority in our everyday lives. Exercise, relaxation, social interaction, and engaging in hobbies are not just self-care practices, they are acts of self-value and self-prioritization. They support and revitalize the body, mind, and soul. Through prioritizing self-care and planning time for rejuvenating activities, we can avert burnout, lessen stress, and improve our general state of well-being. In addition, important components of self-care that can support us in maintaining resilience and balance in the face of life's obstacles include establishing boundaries, saying no to unreasonable requests, and engaging in self-compassion exercises.

Enhancing daily routines also entails developing healthy habits and behaviors supporting long-term well-being. Automatic actions that are frequently carried out without conscious thought are called habits. By deliberately cultivating beneficial habits like consistent exercise, a balanced diet, mindfulness training, and enough sleep, we may boost our general well-being, improve our physical and mental health, and have more energy. It's critical to begin small and develop these habits gradually over time, integrating them into our everyday schedules until they come naturally to us.

In summary, creating more efficient daily routines is an excellent method to increase output, effectiveness, and general well-being. We can make daily routines that support our goals and aspirations by establishing a morning routine, setting priorities for tasks and goals, incorporating regular breaks and downtime, practicing mindfulness and presence, optimizing physical environments and workspaces, putting self-care and well-being first, and developing positive habits. We may optimize our potential, elevate our level of happiness, and lead more satisfying lives by deliberately selecting our actions and modifying our everyday routines.

Building Better Habits Incrementally

Emphasizes tiny, lasting changes over time. This approach stresses the need for steady development and consistency over large-scale attempts or ambitious goals when bringing about long-lasting change. People can develop healthy habits that contributing to long-term success and fulfillment by breaking down bigger goals into smaller, more manageable steps and incorporating new behaviors into everyday routines.

Starting small is a fundamental idea of the gradual habit-building approach. It's more productive to start with little, doable steps rather than attempting to make significant lifestyle changes simultaneously. This could be making a daily commitment to exercise for just five minutes or increasing the amount of water you drink in the morning. People can gain momentum and progressively raise the complexity of their behaviors over time by beginning with tiny, doable steps. By establishing attainable goals, this strategy lessens the fear of change and increases the chance of success.

Moreover, developing improved habits gradually requires consistency. Adopting a new behavior occasionally is insufficient; it must become a regular aspect of everyday life. People strengthen the neural connections in their brains linked to behavior by repeatedly performing it over time, which makes the behavior more automatic and ingrained. The idea of "habit stacking," which entails tying a new habit to an old one, lends credence to this idea. Someone might combine flossing with an existing practice, like cleaning their teeth, to start flossing every night. People can enhance the possibility of sticking to the new behavior and facilitate the easy establishment of habits by associating it with an already-established routine.

Furthermore, it takes persistence and patience to create better behaviors gradually. It takes time for change to occur, and obstacles will inevitably arise. People must embrace a growth attitude, seeing obstacles as chances for improvement and education rather than as justifications to give up. By redefining setbacks as transient impediments and emphasizing advancement over perfection, people can sustain their drive and remain dedicated to their objectives despite the difficulty.

Apart from beginning small and being consistent, people must track their success and modify their strategy as necessary. This may be documenting everyday habits and monitoring progress over time with a notebook or a habit-tracking app. People can find opportunities for improvement and make the required routine adjustments by periodically analyzing their habits and assessing what is and isn't working. Long-term success depends on this process of self-reflection and adaptation, which keeps people moving in the right direction.

Moreover, self-acceptance and self-compassion are necessary for gradually forming healthy behaviors. It's normal for people to encounter obstacles and find it challenging to stick with new routines, but punishing themselves for imagined shortcomings will not help them advance. Instead, people should be compassionate and sympathetic toward themselves, acknowledging that transformation requires time and work. Those who practice self-compassion and forgiveness can develop resilience and keep a positive outlook even when faced with difficulties.

Making the most of accountability and support systems is crucial in gradually forming better habits. Setting and keeping goals with friends, family, or a support group can help with accountability, motivation, and encouragement. Furthermore, joining a group of like-minded people or collaborating with an accountability buddy can provide outside validation and support in keeping people accountable for their actions. On their path to forming better habits, people can improve their odds of success and maintain their motivation by surrounding themselves with supportive people and asking for help.

Additionally, to gradually develop better habits, people must recognize their values and match their habits with their long-term objectives. By defining their goals and the reasons behind their desire to make changes, people can develop a strong sense of motivation and purpose that will keep them going in the face of obstacles and failure. Through reflection and goal-setting, people may give their habits a clear direction and ensure they align with their beliefs and objectives.

Furthermore, acknowledging and appreciating small victories along the way is essential to gradually forming improved habits. Instead of delaying celebration until a goal is entirely accomplished, people should recognize and applaud minor victories and accomplishments. This could be rewarding themselves with a small treat when they meet a mini-goal or expressing pride and accomplishment in their efforts and growth. People reinforce positive behaviors, gain confidence, and gain momentum toward their bigger goals when celebrating their achievements.

To sum up, gradually developing healthier habits is a potent personal growth strategy that stresses gradual, manageable adjustments. People can develop healthy habits that lead to long-term success and fulfillment by starting small, being consistent, exercising patience and perseverance, monitoring progress, practicing self-compassion, utilizing accountability and support, aligning habits with values, and celebrating progress. This method acknowledges that success results from persistent effort, persistence, and self-awareness and that transformation is lengthy. People can modify their lives and make long-lasting progress by adopting the concepts of progressive habit-building.

CHAPTER V

Health and Wellness

Applying Kaizen to Fitness Goals

A systematic and long-lasting strategy for accomplishing health and wellness goals is to apply Kaizen concepts to exercise objectives. Kaizen, which originates from the Japanese concept of continuous development, stresses making gradual, tiny adjustments over time to promote advancement and guarantee long-term success. Regarding fitness, Kaizen urges people to embrace a mindset that emphasizes consistency, slow progress, and long-term lifestyle adjustments. This section will examine the benefits of applying Kaizen concepts to fitness goals, workable implementation tactics, and real-world case studies of people who have successfully transformed their health and fitness through practice.

Applying Kaizen to fitness objectives has several advantages, encouraging sustainability and consistency. Kaizen urges people to make tiny, attainable adjustments to their living routines and behaviors rather than chasing significant changes or quick cures. Individuals can create long-lasting habits more likely to keep by gradually and incrementally approaching fitness. Kaizen encourages people to focus on regular, tiny acts that, over time, add to significant changes in health and wellness, such as exercising every day, eating healthier, or getting enough sleep.

Furthermore, implementing Kaizen to fitness objectives might assist people in overcoming typical obstacles, including a lack of drive, time restraints, or a fear of failing. Kaizen helps people take action and move forward despite obstacles or failures by breaking down more ambitious fitness goals into minor, more doable activities. For instance, instead of aiming high and expecting to lose fifty pounds quickly, people could concentrate on more manageable objectives like working out for thirty minutes every day or cutting back on sugar-filled drinks. Individuals can sustain long-term motivation and commitment to fitness goals through Kaizen, which emphasizes progress over perfection and modest victories.

Applying Kaizen to fitness objectives also fosters a growth attitude, necessary for conquering challenges and succeeding. A growth mindset is distinguished from a fixed mindset by the conviction that aptitudes and competencies may be acquired with diligence and persistence. People with a growth mindset are more inclined to see difficulties as chances for improvement and learning rather than as insurmountable roadblocks. For instance, people with a growth mindset are more inclined to look for new tactics, try various techniques, and keep going after their objectives until they are met rather than giving up when they hit a plateau in their fitness progress.

Applying Kaizen to fitness objectives motivates people to take a comprehensive approach to well-being and health rather than concentrating on performance indicators or outward looks. Although gaining muscle mass or losing weight may be popular fitness objectives, Kaizen encourages people to think about other facets of health and well-being, such as mental wellness, stress reduction, sleep hygiene, and general lifestyle choices. By adopting a more holistic perspective on health and wellness, people can create a more sustainable and well-balanced workout regimen that enhances their overall health and quality of life.

Setting SMART (Specific, Measurable, Achievable, Relevant, Time-bound) goals, breaking down more complex objectives into smaller, more manageable tasks, routinely monitoring progress, and making necessary adjustments to methods based on input and outcomes are all practical ways to apply Kaizen to fitness goals. For instance, instead of aiming for the general objective of "getting in shape," people can establish more precise and quantifiable objectives like "walking for 30 minutes, five days a week" or "eating a serving of vegetables with every meal." People can gain momentum and move closer to their fitness goals by breaking down bigger goals into more minor, manageable chores.

There are numerous real-world instances of people applying Kaizen to their fitness objectives with success. Take Sarah's example, a working mother with a full schedule who found exercising challenging. Sarah decided to concentrate on implementing tiny, long-lasting adjustments to her everyday schedule rather than attempting to squeeze in lengthy workouts or tight diets. She began by taking quick walks during her lunch breaks, and with time, she increased the length and intensity of her workouts. She also made minor dietary adjustments, like eating fewer portions and substituting healthier snacks for sweet ones. Sarah experienced neither overwhelm nor deprivation as she lost weight, gained more energy and enhanced her general health and well-being by embracing a Kaizen approach to fitness.

Likewise, let us examine the case of John, a middle-aged guy whose lousy eating habits and sedentary lifestyle contributed to his chronic health problems and low self-esteem. John decided to concentrate on making one tiny adjustment at a time rather than attempting to restructure his way of life all at once completely. He began by adding quick, daily workouts to his schedule, and as he gained strength and endurance, he steadily increased the length and intensity of his workouts. Additionally, he made minor dietary adjustments, such as increasing the number of fruits and vegetables in his meals and reducing the number of processed foods and sugary drinks. John's persistent efforts eventually paid off, and he could reduce his weight, increase his fitness level, and regain his self-esteem and confidence.

In summary, implementing Kaizen concepts into fitness targets provides a systematic and long-lasting way to reach wellness and health goals. People can surmount typical obstacles through a commitment to consistency, incremental enhancement, and long-term lifestyle modifications, cultivate a growth mentality, and attain sustained success in their fitness endeavors. People can achieve steady progress toward their fitness targets and enjoy increased health, well-being, and quality of life by using doable tactics, including setting SMART goals, monitoring progress frequently, and modifying strategies depending on input and outcomes.

Enhancing Nutrition with Minor Adjustments

Making minor dietary adjustments can significantly impact one's health and well-being. Making modest, long-lasting dietary adjustments provides a welcome diversion from the extremes and fad diets that so frequently characterize discussions about nutrition. This approach to nutrition is based on the ideas of Kaizen, which encourage continual development through tiny, gradual stages. Rather than attempting radical overhauls or restrictive diets, this method emphasizes minor improvements to eating patterns over time. This section will examine the advantages of implementing minor dietary adjustments, workable methods for doing so, and case studies of people who have effectively enhanced their health and well-being using this strategy.

Making tiny, sustainable changes to enhance nutrition has many advantages, one of which is that it encourages long-term success. In contrast to severe or crash diets, which frequently cause temporary weight loss followed by gain, gradual, sustained modifications to eating patterns can result in long-term gains in well-being and health. People can adopt better eating habits more likely to last over time by concentrating on minor, steady improvements, enhancing their quality of life, and improving their health.

Additionally, individuals can overcome common obstacles to healthy eating, such as lack of time, motivation, or understanding, by implementing minor modifications that increase nutrition. Instead of trying to alter their diet all at once drastically, people should concentrate on making one tiny adjustment at a time, such as increasing the number of vegetables they eat or substituting sugar-filled beverages with water. Even in the face of difficulties or setbacks, people can maintain momentum and make steady progress toward their dietary goals by breaking larger goals down into more minor, more achievable activities.

Additionally, implementing minor adjustments to increase nutrition inspires people to eat more flexibly and balanced. This method encourages people to listen to their bodies, follow their hunger and fullness cues, and make decisions that support their physical and emotional well-being rather than putting a lot of emphasis on rigid rules or meal plans. People can have a healthy relationship with food and adopt a more positive outlook on eating by allowing themselves to enjoy various meals in moderation.

Realistic approaches to improving nutrition with tiny adjustments include establishing clear, attainable objectives, like consuming one extra serving of vegetables daily or preparing one new nutritious dish per week. By establishing specific, quantifiable goals, people may monitor their development and maintain their motivation to improve. People might also gradually alter their eating habits by eating fewer portions, consuming more whole meals, or consuming fewer processed foods and sugary snacks. A gradual approach to diet modification allows people to develop healthier habits that are more likely to stick over time.

Numerous real-world instances of people who have successfully improved their diet by making minor adjustments. Take Jane as an example. She was a busy working mother who found it challenging to find time to cook her family healthful meals in her busy schedule. Jane decided to concentrate on implementing one tiny adjustment at a time rather than trying to alter her family's diet all at once drastically. She began by increasing the number of fruits and vegetables in her family's meals and then gradually cutting back on the number of processed foods and sugary snacks they ate. Her family's health and well-being significantly improved over time due to these modest adjustments, enhancing digestion and giving them more energy and vigor.

In a similar vein, let's look at the instance of John, a middle-aged guy whose bad eating habits contributed to his obesity and associated health problems. Instead of starting a tight diet or rigorous workout program, John concentrated on making tiny, long-lasting adjustments to his eating habits. He began by eating fewer portions and increasing the number of complete foods in his diet, such as fruits, vegetables, lean proteins, and whole grains. He also tried to cut back on the number of sugar-filled snacks and drinks and increase his water intake. With time, these modest adjustments assisted John in lowering his blood sugar levels, losing weight, and lowering his chance of developing chronic illness.

To sum up, implementing minor adjustments to improve diet provides a long-term and practical way to improve health and well-being. Focusing on minor, gradual dietary habit modifications can help people get beyond common obstacles to eating healthily, have a more flexible and balanced approach to food, and meet their nutrition objectives in the long run. People may develop healthier behaviors that promote their general health and well-being and enhance their quality of life and energy by utilizing doable tactics like focusing on minor, incremental adjustments and creating clear, attainable goals.

Mental Health and Stress Management

Effective stress management and mental health are: essential components of total well-being, impacting all facets of our lives, including relationships, productivity at work, physical health and overall quality of life.

It is crucial to prioritize mental health and create efficient stress management techniques in today's fast-paced, high-demanding world. This section will discuss the importance of stress management and mental health, the effects of stress on physical and psychological health, doable methods for reducing stress and fostering mental health, and the part resilience and self-care play in preserving mental health at its best.

The first and most important thing to understand is how important mental health is to general health and well-being. Our emotional, psychological, and social well-being are all a part of our mental health, which affects our thoughts, feelings, and actions daily. Good mental health is a condition of total well-being in which people can manage life's stressors, work effectively, and give back to their communities. It goes beyond simply being free from mental illness. Maintaining resilience, controlling stress, and leading a happy and meaningful life all depend on placing a high priority on mental health.

Stress, a normal and unavoidable aspect of life, can be seen as the body's reaction to pressure or obligations. While a certain amount of stress can be beneficial, motivating us to act and overcome obstacles, prolonged or severe stress can be detrimental to our mental and physical well-being. It's important to remember that we have the power to identify the signs and symptoms of stress and develop effective coping mechanisms. This understanding and proactive approach can empower us to safeguard our mental health and avoid the detrimental effects of ongoing stress.

Proactive steps to develop resilience and coping mechanisms to handle stress when it occurs are two valuable approaches for reducing stress and fostering mental health. Developing the capacity to overcome obstacles, recover from setbacks, and flourish in the face of adversity is the process of building resilience. Developing social support networks, keeping an optimistic attitude, getting regular exercise, and using mindfulness and relaxation techniques are among the strategies that can help achieve this. Deep breathing exercises, progressive muscle relaxation, guided imagery, and cognitive-behavioral approaches, including problem-solving and reframing negative beliefs, are some coping mechanisms for stress management.

Moreover, effective stress management and the maintenance of optimum mental health are deeply rooted in self-care. It's not just a luxury, but a necessity. Prioritizing behaviors and activities that support our physical, emotional, and mental health is a way of showing ourselves that we are important and deserving of well-being. These behaviors and activities, such as getting enough sleep, maintaining a healthy diet, exercising frequently, spending time with loved ones, pursuing interests and hobbies, and establishing boundaries to safeguard our privacy, are all acts of self-care. We can effectively manage stress, build resilience, and preserve our general well-being by making time for these things.

It's also critical to understand that asking for professional support and assistance is a show of strength rather than weakness. Speaking with a mental health professional can offer you the support, direction, and tools you need to manage and recover if you are dealing with stress, anxiety, depression, or other mental health issues. Support groups, therapy, and counseling can provide a private, safe environment to explore your feelings and ideas, acquire coping mechanisms, and create more efficient stress management techniques. For those with more severe or ongoing mental health problems, prescription drugs and other therapies might also be suggested.

In summary, stress reduction and mental health are critical elements of total well-being that impact all facets of our lives. Resilience, stress management, and purposeful and meaningful life depend on prioritizing mental health, creating practical stress-reduction plans, and engaging in self-care. By identifying stress indicators and symptoms, developing resilience in self-care, and providing professional assistance when required, people can safeguard their mental health, improve their overall well-being, and prosper in today's fast-paced and demanding world.

CHAPTER VI

Personal Development

Setting and Achieving Personal Goals

Establishing and achieving goals is one of the most critical components of success, personal development, and progress. Setting specific, attainable goals gives direction, drive, and a feeling of purpose, whether pursuing personal aspirations, job progress, academic excellence, or fitness and health objectives. This section will discuss the significance of establishing and accomplishing personal goals, the goal-setting process, typical roadblocks to goal achievement, how to get beyond these roadblocks, and the contribution of tenacity and resilience to success.

Primarily, establishing personal objectives is crucial for clarifying our objectives and devising a plan of action to reach them. Setting goals gives us direction and clarity, giving us something to strive for. Setting SMART (specific, measurable, attainable, relevant, and time-bound) goals helps people focus their efforts, make clear what they want to achieve, and monitor their progress over time. Establishing measurable objectives is the first step to reaching your goals:

- Learning a new skill
- Finishing your degree
- Moving forward in your career
- Getting more physically fit

Furthermore, reaching personal objectives requires thorough preparation, tenacity, and devotion. Setting goals entails determining priorities, evaluating strengths and weaknesses, dividing more complex objectives into minor, more doable activities, and creating a completion schedule.

A plan of action and reasonable expectations can help people stay motivated to reach their goals and improve their chances of success. Furthermore, by revisiting and reevaluating goals regularly, people may monitor their progress, make necessary modifications, and continue on their path to success.

Nevertheless, despite the advantages of goal planning, many people need help to accomplish their objectives because of typical roadblocks, including self-doubt, procrastination, lack of desire, and fear of failing. It takes self-awareness, resiliency, and determination to overcome these obstacles in the face of difficulties. Procrastination can be overcome, and motivation can be increased by dividing goals into smaller, more doable tasks, establishing deadlines, fostering a positive environment, and recognizing accomplishments. Furthermore, developing a growth mindset—which prioritizes learning and development above fixed abilities— may support people in overcoming self-doubt and failure-related anxiety so they can continue to be resilient while pursuing their objectives.

In addition, reaching personal objectives frequently necessitates overcoming outside barriers like conflicting agendas, time restraints, and financial limits. Setting priorities for your work, using time management techniques, enlisting the help of others, and taking advantage of chances and resources are some strategies for getting beyond these challenges. Furthermore, flexibility and adaptability in the face of unforeseen difficulties enable people to overcome setbacks and hurdles and progress toward their objectives.

Reaching personal goals is not just about overcoming barriers, but also about building resilience and tenacity in the face of failures and disappointments. Failure and obstacles are inevitable in the pursuit of goals, but it's how we handle these setbacks that ultimately determines our success. By maintaining an optimistic mindset, taking responsibility for our actions, and emerging from hardships stronger and more determined, we can develop resilience and continue our journey toward our goals with renewed vigor and self-assurance.

Consider the inspiring journey of Sarah, a single mother who was determined to complete her college education to secure a better future for her children. Despite facing financial hardships, childcare responsibilities, and academic challenges, Sarah's unwavering commitment to her SMART goals, support from her social circle, and resilience in the face of obstacles led her to graduate and pave the way for a brighter future for her family.

Analogously, take John's example. John was a budding businessman who had aspirations of launching his own company. John was determined to achieve his objective and put in much effort to see it through, even though he needed more finances and skills. John successfully launched his business and realized his long-held dream of being a prosperous entrepreneur by setting clear, attainable goals, looking for mentoring and advice from seasoned professionals, and overcoming obstacles with resiliency and dedication.

In conclusion, a key component of success, personal development, and progress is establishing and completing personal goals. People can realize their aspirations and design their lives by making specific, attainable goals, developing a plan of action, getting beyond challenges, and strengthening their resilience and tenacity. Even though achieving goals can be complex and full of detours, the benefits of success—such as contentment, fulfillment, and personal development—make the effort worthwhile. People may realize their dreams and succeed in all aspects of their lives with meticulous planning, tenacity, and unshakable dedication.

Continuous Learning and Skill Acquisition

In the fast-paced world we live in, the acquisition of new skills and the commitment to lifelong learning are not just beneficial, but essential for both personal and professional growth. In an era marked by rapid technological advancements, globalization, and economic uncertainty, those who embrace a growth-oriented mindset and actively pursue lifelong learning are not just better equipped to thrive, but also to lead. This section will delve into the value of lifelong learning and skill development, the myriad advantages they offer, practical strategies for integrating learning into our daily lives, and the pivotal role that lifelong learning plays in shaping our professional and personal development.

At the heart of professional success in today's competitive and ever-evolving workforce lies the commitment to continuous education and skill development. Those who fail to update their skills and adapt to the changing demands of their sectors and job roles risk being left behind or rendered obsolete. By embracing a culture of continuous learning, individuals can stay abreast of emerging trends, technologies, and best practices, thereby enhancing their flexibility and agility and positioning themselves for success in a job market that is in a constant state of flux.

Furthermore, lifelong learning and skill development promote fulfillment and personal growth. Acquiring new abilities pertaining to a person's career, interests, or pastimes can extend perspectives, spark innovation, and boost self-assurance. People broaden their horizons, better grasp the world around them, and find new hobbies and interests that improve their lives when they push themselves to leave their comfort zones and pick up new skills and knowledge.

Furthermore, lifelong learning and skill development enable people to follow their professional dreams and realize their goals. People who invest in their continuous learning are better positioned to take advantage of growth and advancement possibilities, whether looking to advance within their present organization or move to a different area or business. People can improve their worth to employers, raise their earning potential, and experience more job satisfaction and fulfillment by learning new skills and knowledge related to their chosen professional path.

Moreover, innovation and economic expansion are facilitated by ongoing education and skill development. Organizations that prioritize learning and development are better able to innovate, adapt, and stay competitive in a global economy that is becoming increasingly competitive. By promoting an environment that values ongoing education and the acquisition of new competencies, companies may unleash the creativity and inventiveness of their personnel, resulting in increased economic growth and innovation.

Setting learning objectives, making an organized learning plan, and using a range of resources and learning opportunities are all sensible methods for implementing continuous learning into daily living. Establishing specific, attainable learning objectives gives people a road map for their learning process and keeps them motivated and engaged. Choosing pertinent learning materials, setting aside time for learning activities, and implementing accountability measures to guarantee success are all part of creating an organized learning strategy. People can also benefit from various resources and educational opportunities, such as professional development programs, books, podcasts, workshops, seminars, and online courses.

It is also impossible to overestimate the importance of ongoing education for professional and personal development. People can live more fulfilled lives, reach their goals, and realize their full potential by actively seeking learning and skill-acquisition opportunities. Continuous learning empowers people to flourish in a constantly changing world, adapt to change, and take advantage of possibilities. This includes learning new languages, gaining technical skills, gaining professional certifications, and developing leadership qualities.

In conclusion, in today's quickly evolving world, skill development and ongoing learning are crucial elements of both professional and personal growth. People can maintain relevance, competitiveness, and fulfillment in their personal and professional lives by adopting a lifelong learning mindset and actively seeking opportunities to acquire new skills and knowledge. Continuous learning enables people to reach their objectives, realize their potential, and have more rewarding and happy lives—whether seeking career success, personal development, or broadening their horizons.

Time Management and Productivity Hacks

To effectively and efficiently navigate the pressures of modern life and accomplish our goals, mastering time management and productivity is not just vital, it's empowering. Success in both the personal and professional spheres is within our control, even in today's fast-paced world of constant diversions and demands on our time. This section will discuss the value of productivity and time management, typical problems people run into, practical tips and techniques for increasing productivity and time management, and the advantages of developing these abilities in a variety of contexts.

First and foremost, it is impossible to overestimate the significance of productivity and time management. Since time is a limited resource, how we decide to divide and use it affects our capacity to complete activities, reach objectives, and have happy, meaningful lives. We may prioritize tasks, reduce distractions, and concentrate on activities supporting our beliefs and goals when we practice effective time management. Similarly, productivity is necessary to maximize output and successfully and efficiently accomplish desired results. Through process optimization, time-saving measures, and applying technologies and strategies to boost productivity, we can complete tasks more quickly and succeed in our activities more.

However, many people struggle with managing their time and being productive due to a variety of issues, such as disorganization, overwhelm, and procrastination. The good news is that these are all challenges that can be overcome. Effective time management is often hindered by procrastination, as people put off crucial tasks in favor of less taxing or more pleasurable activities. Overwhelm can cause people to feel immobilized by the amount of work and obligations they have to complete. Furthermore, disorganization can result in inefficiencies and time loss. But with the right strategies, these challenges can be turned into opportunities for growth and improvement.

People may use many tips and tricks to increase productivity and time management. Time-blocking, which includes setting aside specific blocks of time for particular tasks or activities, is one helpful tactic. People can reduce interruptions and increase productivity by blocking uninterrupted time for concentrated work. Similarly, people can stay focused and prevent burnout using the Pomodoro Technique, which includes working for brief, concentrated intervals followed by short pauses.

Furthermore, productivity and efficient time management depend on prioritization. People can better manage their time and resources by distinguishing between urgent and vital jobs and those not as important. For example, the Eisenhower Matrix is a helpful tool for setting task priorities according to their significance and urgency, allowing people to concentrate on those with the most significant effects. Furthermore, grouping related jobs into batches can facilitate workflow optimization and reduce context switching, which boosts productivity and efficiency.

Furthermore, time management and increased production depend on efficient organization. People can minimize distractions, decrease clutter, and streamline their workflow using task, information, and resource organization systems. People may stay on top of assignments, deadlines, and appointments using digital tools like note-taking apps, calendar applications, and task management apps. This way, everything gets noticed. Similarly, developing a daily or weekly planning schedule can assist people in setting objectives, setting priorities, and creating a successful plan.

Automation and technology can also help people become more productive and save time. Automation software, text expanders, and email filters are some tools that can reduce repetitive work and free up time for more critical projects. Similarly, assigning or outsourcing non-essential work can free up time for people to concentrate on high-impact endeavors that support their values and goals. People can be more productive and efficient in their personal and professional lives by utilizing technology and assigning work wisely.

Moreover, general well-being and productivity depend on preserving a positive work-life balance. Fatigue and burnout can reduce output and result in lower performance and pleasure. As a result, it's critical that people prioritize taking care of themselves, establish limits, and schedule time for leisure activities and rest. Long-term stress reduction, productivity maintenance, and battery recharging can be achieved by taking pauses, meditating, and partaking in joyful and fulfilling activities.

In addition, maintaining relevance and competitiveness requires ongoing learning and skill development in today's world of rapid global change. People can increase their effectiveness and productivity by investing in continuing education and professional development. This allows them to gain new knowledge and abilities. Whether through traditional schooling, online courses, workshops, or self-directed learning, people can learn continuously to adapt to changing circumstances, take advantage of new possibilities, and accomplish their objectives more successfully.

To sum up, time management and productivity are critical abilities for juggling the rigors of contemporary life and accomplishing our objectives effectively and efficiently. People can accomplish more in less time and succeed more in their personal and professional interests by learning the art of time management, limiting distractions, and increasing productivity. People may use several techniques and productivity boosters to improve their time management and productivity, whether through efficient prioritization, organizing, using technology, or upholding an excellent work-life balance. People can achieve more success and fulfillment by embracing and implementing these strategies into their everyday routines.

CHAPTER VII

Kaizen in Business

Implementing Kaizen in Corporate Culture

Kaizen implementation in corporate culture is a revolutionary method of organizational reform that prioritizes ongoing minor adjustments and full employee participation. Kaizen ("change for the better") is a systematic strategy to identify and implement minor, progressive improvements in processes, systems, and practices to promote efficiency, productivity, and quality. It is derived from the Japanese idea of continuous improvement. This section will examine the fundamentals of Kaizen, the advantages of incorporating Kaizen into corporate culture, implementation tactics, and actual case studies of businesses that have used Kaizen to increase performance and competitiveness significantly.

Fundamentally, Kaizen is founded on several important ideas, such as an emphasis on ongoing development, human dignity, and a collaborative and team-oriented culture. Continuous improvement means not waiting for significant issues to happen but regularly making tiny, gradual adjustments to systems and processes. Through consistently pursuing opportunities for enhancement and employee involvement in the process, establishments can foster a culture of ongoing education and creativity. Respect for individuals promotes cooperation, empowerment, and participation at all levels by acknowledging the worth of each individual inside the company. Open communication, mutual trust, and shared accountability for accomplishing corporate goals are all fostered by a culture of cooperation and teamwork.

Organizations can gain a lot from implementing Kaizen in corporate culture, such as higher productivity, quality, and efficiency, as well as improved morale and employee engagement, less waste and inefficiency, and greater profitability and competitiveness. Through employee empowerment to discover and execute process improvements, organizations may leverage their staff's pooled knowledge, skills, and creativity, resulting in increased innovation and sustained growth. Additionally, by promoting a culture of ongoing learning and development, businesses can better adjust to shifting consumer demands, market dynamics, and technology breakthroughs, securing long-term survival and success.

Kaizen can only be successfully incorporated into corporate culture with a systematic approach and a strong commitment from the leadership. Establishing a clear vision and understanding of Kaizen principles and methodologies, training and supporting staff at all levels, setting goals and objectives for improvement, and cultivating a positive and empowering work environment are all crucial steps in the implementation process. Organizations must also guarantee that staff members have the time, freedom, and encouragement to fully engage in the process by providing the infrastructure, tools, and resources required to support Kaizen projects.

Numerous real-world instances of businesses have effectively incorporated Kaizen into their corporate cultures. Take Toyota as an example. Toyota is one of the top automakers in the world and has a long history of invention and constant improvement. Based on the ideas of Kaizen, Toyota's production system—often referred to as "Lean Manufacturing" or "Toyota Production System"—has been extensively implemented by businesses worldwide. Toyota has achieved extraordinary productivity, quality, and efficiency advances by enabling workers to discover and address problems on the factory floor. This has allowed Toyota to become the industry leader in quality and productivity in the automotive sector.

Analogously, please consider the situation of Amazon, the massive online retailer that has embraced Kaizen concepts to promote efficiency and creativity in its business practices. Amazon's unwavering pursuit of operational efficiency and customer satisfaction indicates its ongoing experimentation and improvement culture. Amazon's approach to Kaizen has helped it stay ahead of the competition and hold its position as a global leader in e-commerce and technology, from its emphasis on data-driven decision-making and automation to its dedication to employee empowerment and autonomy.

In summary, incorporating Kaizen into corporate culture gives businesses a strong foundation for fostering innovation, growth, and continual improvement. Organizations may harness their workforce's collective knowledge and creativity to drive long-term gains in performance and competitiveness by cultivating a culture of empowerment, cooperation, and ongoing learning. The benefits of pursuing Kaizen, which include higher productivity, quality, efficiency, improved employee morale and engagement, and increased profitability and competitiveness, make the trip worthwhile even though it may take some time and effort. In today's fast-paced and cutthroat business world, businesses can successfully embrace Kaizen and realize their full potential for success by focusing on people and processes, demonstrating outstanding leadership, and being committed.

Case Studies of Successful Kaizen Implementations

Adequate Kaizen implementation case studies offer insightful information on how continuous improvement concepts are applied in various businesses and organizations. These cases show how applying Kaizen techniques can result in notable gains in output, effectiveness, quality, and worker happiness. We may identify important tactics, difficulties, and results related to implementing Kaizen initiatives by looking through these case studies. We can also get ideas for our improvement projects.

Toyota's production system is a noteworthy illustration of a successful Kaizen implementation that transformed the automotive industry. The Toyota Production System (TPS), which is Toyota's approach to Kaizen, strongly emphasizes waste reduction, continual improvement, and respect for people. Toyota has made impressive progress in quality, cost, and lead time by allowing employees to find and fix issues early on. For instance, Toyota has been able to lower inventory levels, cut waste, and react swiftly to consumer demand by embracing a pull-based production system and Just-In-Time (JIT) manufacturing principles.

Another noteworthy example of a successful Kaizen implementation is from the healthcare sector, namely, Seattle, Washington's Virginia Mason Medical Center. Virginia Mason started a Kaizen initiative to change its procedures and organizational culture to improve patient safety, care quality, and operational effectiveness. Using programs like daily huddles and Rapid Process Improvement Workshops (RPIWs), Virginia Mason helped frontline employees recognize and resolve problems in real-time. The medical center enhanced patient outcomes, decreased medical errors, and streamlined operations as a result. Since then, Virginia Mason's Kaizen success has motivated other healthcare institutions to embrace similar techniques for continuous improvement.

Additionally, many instances in the industrial industry of successful Kaizen implementations have resulted in notable increases in quality and productivity. The tale of Wiremold, a producer of electrical wire gear, is one such instance. To resurrect its operations in the face of fierce competition and diminishing profitability, Wiremold turned to Kaizen. Reducing Reduced lead times, enhanced product quality, and boosted customer satisfaction were all achieved by Wiremold through lean manufacturing principles and employee empowerment. Through its successful Kaizen journey, the company regained its competitive advantage and developed a continuous improvement culture that continues to inspire innovation and quality.

Apart from the manufacturing and healthcare sectors, there are also noteworthy instances of practical Kaizen implementations in the service business. For example, McDonald's has improved operations and customer service by applying Kaizen principles. Through process standardization, workflow streamlining, and staff empowerment, McDonald's has improved efficiency, minimized waste, and provided consumers with an enhanced eating experience. From rearranging drive-thru to streamlining kitchen layouts, McDonald's has shown how Kaizen can revolutionize an organization and help it stay ahead of the competition.

In addition, the hospitality sector has adopted Kaizen's ideas to improve visitor experiences and operational effectiveness. The Ritz-Carlton Hotel Company, which is well-known for its first-rate service and opulent lodgings, has used Kaizen techniques to uphold its exacting standards of quality. The Ritz-Carlton has been able to provide individualized service, anticipate guests' requirements, and surpass expectations by cultivating a culture of continuous improvement and allowing staff to take ownership of visitor happiness. Every facet of the hotel's operations, including housekeeping procedures and front desk operations, is continuously optimized using Kaizen.

Furthermore, successful Kaizen implementations in the technology industry have produced innovation and a competitive edge. For instance, software development firms like Google and Microsoft have used Kaizen concepts to enhance their product development procedures and promote an innovative culture. These companies have achieved increased productivity and quality product delivery by applying Agile principles and encouraging experimentation. Teams continually iterate and improve their work through sprint planning, daily stand-up meetings, and retrospective reviews, leading to higher customer satisfaction and market success.

To summarize, case studies of practical Kaizen implementations offer insightful guidance and motivation to businesses looking to enhance their operations and output. It has been demonstrated that applying the kaizen concepts to the manufacturing, healthcare, service, or technology sectors can result in notable production, quality, and worker engagement gains. Through employee empowerment, the promotion of a continuous improvement culture, and the adoption of Lean concepts, firms can attain long-term success and sustain a competitive advantage in today's ever-changing business landscape. The success stories of Google, Microsoft, McDonald's, Toyota, Virginia Mason, Wiremold, and The Ritz-Carlton serve as excellent examples of continuous improvement and highlight the transformative power of Kaizen.

Overcoming Resistance to Change

One of the biggest obstacles companies must overcome when introducing new programs, tactics, or procedures is resistance to change. Today's dynamic and competitive business world is characterized by constant change, fueled by several reasons, such as market disruptions, evolving consumer demands, and technological breakthroughs. Though there may be advantages to change, resistance frequently develops for several reasons, such as fear of the unknown, a sense of losing control, and the perception of dangers to one's job security or status quo. This section will look at the reasons behind resistance to change, how it affects organizations, how to get past resistance, and how leadership plays a vital part in making change projects successful.

Fear of the unknown is one of the main factors contributing to reluctance to change. Because humans have an innate desire for consistency and predictability, resistance to change can be sparked by ambiguity about its potential effects. Workers can worry that new changes will interfere with their routines, force them to pick up new skills or jeopardize their job security. People may also oppose change if they believe it would affect their sense of self, level of skill, or standing within the company. Through open communication, education, and support, organizations can help employees overcome their anxieties and gain the confidence to welcome change by recognizing and addressing these fears.

Furthermore, ignorance of the rationale for the suggested changes and their possible advantages may also cause resistance to change. If workers believe a change is being forced upon them without sufficient cause or explanation, they may oppose it. Organizations must thus communicate clearly and honestly regarding the need for change, the goals it aims to accomplish, and the expected advantages for both the company and its constituents. Organizations can encourage employee buy-in and commitment to change by involving them in the change process, asking for their opinions, and offering chances for discussion and explanation.

Perceived loss of autonomy or control can also be a source of resistance to change. Workers who want to keep their independence and control over their work may oppose change if they believe it is being forced upon them without their consent or cooperation. As a result, businesses must include their staff members in the change process and provide them the authority to make decisions and solve problems. Organizations may lessen resistance and promote ownership and accountability for change by asking frontline staff members for their opinions, involving them in the planning and executing of change projects, and giving them opportunities to share their knowledge and ideas.

Organizational cultures and leadership philosophies that are themselves resistant to change can also worsen resistance to change. Firmly ingrained cultural norms, attitudes, and beliefs can occasionally exacerbate resistance to change, making it challenging for businesses to adjust and develop in response to shifting market conditions. Leaders who resist change or do not effectively convey the purpose and reasoning behind the change may also unintentionally fuel employee resistance. To support practical change projects, companies must evaluate their culture and leadership practices and pinpoint the areas that require modification.

Developing open lines of communication, establishing rapport and trust, offering assistance and resources, and cultivating an environment that values experimentation and learning are all valuable tactics for overcoming resistance to change. Building a shared understanding and commitment to change objectives and addressing misconceptions, anxieties, and worries regarding change depend on effective communication. Organizations should communicate the need for change, its justification, and its anticipated results clearly and consistently. Leaders should also respond to queries and concerns, give chances for communication and cooperation, and actively listen to employee input.

Furthermore, overcoming resistance to change requires developing a rapport and trusting relationship with employees. When workers believe in their leaders and can handle complexity and ambiguity, they are more likely to welcome change. As a result, leaders should actively involve staff members in decision-making and problem-solving processes and exhibit empathy, sincerity, and integrity in their communications and actions. Organizations can foster a supportive work environment where people feel empowered to welcome change and make valuable contributions by establishing relationships based on mutual respect and trust.

Additionally, offering employees resources and support is crucial to assisting them in overcoming change's obstacles and developing the abilities and skills necessary to flourish in novel situations. This could entail offering training and development opportunities to enhance workers' abilities in areas like change management, communication, and problem-solving. Organizations should also make coaching, mentoring, and other assistance available to staff members so they may develop resilience in the face of uncertainty and deal with the psychological and emotional challenges of transition.

Additionally, by encouraging staff members to embrace novel concepts, take calculated chances, and learn from successes and mistakes, businesses can overcome reluctance to change by fostering a culture of learning and experimentation. Organizations may establish a secure and supportive atmosphere where employees are inspired to question the status quo and explore new possibilities by promoting a growth mindset and applauding innovation and creativity. Leaders should set an example of being open to learning and adapting, encourage inquiry and exploration, and honor staff members who contribute to change projects.

Furthermore, overcoming resistance to change and spearheading successful change initiatives depend heavily on the leadership role. A clear vision for change must be expressed by leaders, together with the necessity and significance of the change, to encourage and inspire staff members to accept it. Leaders must set an example for others by acting with compassion, grit, and optimism in the face of uncertainty and misfortune. Leaders should also establish a culture of accountability and continual improvement where change is seen as a chance for personal growth and development. This includes giving staff guidance, resources, and support.

In summary, organizations must overcome resistance to change as a significant obstacle when introducing new programs, tactics, or procedures. Organizations may successfully traverse the challenges of change and promote innovation, growth, and success by comprehending the reasons behind resistance to change, applying effective techniques for overcoming resistance and cultivating a culture of learning and experimentation. Effective leadership is essential for driving change efforts that succeed. Leadership must exhibit empathy, authenticity, and resilience when guiding employees through the change process. Ultimately, companies may position themselves for long-term success and sustainability in today's dynamic and competitive business climate by accepting change as a natural and necessary aspect of organizational evolution.

CHAPTER VIII

Team Dynamics and Leadership

Fostering a Culture of Continuous improvement in Teams
To adapt, innovate, and prosper in today's fast-paced business world, organizations must cultivate a culture of continuous improvement within their teams. People who work in an environment that prioritizes continuous improvement are more inclined to see growth opportunities early on, question the status quo, and strive for excellence in their work. By cultivating a cooperative and encouraging atmosphere that values experimentation, learning, and creativity, teams can improve performance over time, increase employee engagement, and produce better outcomes. This section, which uses examples from various businesses and organizations, examines the essential ideas, tactics, and advantages of encouraging a culture of continuous team improvement.

The foundation of a culture that prioritizes continuous development is the concept of Kaizen, a Japanese ideology that stresses gradual and constant enhancement in every facet of existence. Kaizen pushes people to look for tiny, gradual improvements that add up to significant breakthroughs over time. By cultivating an attitude that prioritizes ongoing education, flexibility, and development, groups can effectively navigate obstacles, grasp chances, and attain enhanced productivity. Furthermore, Kaizen highlights the value of cooperation and teamwork in promoting improvement, understanding that various viewpoints and a team effort are necessary to produce creative solutions and promote significant change.

To promote a culture of continuous development in teams, it's essential to provide a psychologically secure space where people may freely exchange ideas, pose queries, and confront presumptions. A setting in which team members feel free to take chances, voice their thoughts, and be themselves without worrying about criticism or retaliation is known as psychological safety. Studies have indicated that teams exhibiting elevated psychological safety have higher innovation, creativity, and resilience levels. This is attributed to team members feeling encouraged to voice their opinions, take risks, and offer their distinct viewpoints and insights. In addition to demonstrating vulnerability, humility, and openness, leaders are essential in fostering psychological safety because they promote open dialogue, feedback, and communication within the team.

In addition, maintaining a culture of continual improvement necessitates a dedication to lifelong learning and skill advancement. Teams can receive assistance from organizations in this quest by accessing resources, training, and professional development opportunities. Businesses show their dedication to fostering individual growth and advancing group capabilities by investing in staff development. Moreover, companies may develop a flexible, resilient workforce that can spearhead innovation and continual development by encouraging people to gain new information, skills, and competencies.

A crucial element in cultivating a culture of ongoing enhancement is defining unambiguous objectives, measurements, and feedback systems to monitor advancement and gauge achievement. Establishing SMART (specific, measurable, attainable, relevant, and time-bound) goals gives teams a clear focus and direction for their development efforts. Moreover, teams may pinpoint areas for development, recognize accomplishments, and make necessary course corrections by establishing key performance indicators (KPIs) and routinely assessing progress against these measures. Furthermore, giving prompt, helpful feedback enables people to recognize their areas of strength and growth, which empowers them to take proactive measures to enhance their performance and make well-informed decisions.

Moreover, companies must welcome experimentation, creativity, and risk-taking to develop a continual improvement culture. Encouraging teams to test theories, investigate novel concepts, and draw lessons from achievements and setbacks is essential. Organizations may unlock the creative potential of their teams and effect significant change by fostering a culture that values experimentation and promotes innovation. Moreover, companies may foster an atmosphere where people feel encouraged to take measured risks and achieve lofty objectives by promoting a development mentality that sees failure as a normal part of the learning process.

In addition, acknowledging and commemorating accomplishments and significant junctures along the path is essential to cultivating a culture of perpetual enhancement. Celebrating accomplishments promotes morale, motivation, and team cohesion, in addition to reinforcing positive actions and results. Leaders may create a culture of thankfulness and recognition that motivates people to go above and beyond in their pursuit of excellence by recognizing the contributions of team members and expressing appreciation for their efforts. Publicly recognizing accomplishments and disseminating best practices and lessons gained also fosters a culture of continuous improvement within the company, encouraging others to model successful actions and results.

A dedication to openness, responsibility, and empowerment is also necessary to promote a culture of continual improvement. Teams should have easy access to the pertinent data, knowledge, and tools required to lead improvement projects successfully. Furthermore, there should be clear expectations and repercussions for success and failure, and individuals should be held accountable for their actions and contributions to the team's objectives. In addition, teams must be free to decide for themselves and take responsibility for their efforts at improvement, with leaders offering direction, assistance, and resources as required to ensure success.

In addition, cultivating a culture of continuous improvement calls for encouraging a sense of belonging, cooperation, and a common goal among team members. By facilitating chances for team members to work together, exchange knowledge, and provide mutual support, organizations may leverage their teams' combined creativity and intellect to propel innovation and progress. Organizations can also improve team cohesion and morale by cultivating a sense of belonging and camaraderie. This results in a positive atmosphere where people are encouraged to put forth their best efforts because they feel respected, valued, and cherished.

In conclusion, companies looking to innovate, adapt, and thrive in today's cutthroat business world must cultivate a culture of continuous improvement among their staff. Organizations can create a culture that motivates people to pursue excellence and effect meaningful change by adopting the principles of Kaizen, establishing a psychologically safe environment, investing in learning and development, defining clear goals and metrics, welcoming experimentation and innovation, celebrating successes, promoting accountability and transparency, and cultivating a sense of community and collaboration. By working together, having a common goal, and being dedicated to continuous development, teams may reach their maximum potential and provide better outcomes.

Leadership Strategies for Promoting Kaizen

Establishing a culture of continuous improvement in organizations requires leadership tactics that support Kaizen. Kaizen is a Japanese concept that stresses gradual and ongoing improvement in all facets of life and work. Teams need strong leadership to support and mentor teams in their improvement endeavors. To foster an atmosphere where Kaizen principles can flourish, leaders must encourage staff members to proactively seek out areas for improvement, try out novel concepts, and promote change. This section uses examples from prosperous businesses and sectors to examine several leadership techniques for advancing Kaizen.

A crucial leadership tactic for advancing Kaizen involves setting a good example and showcasing a dedication to ongoing development. Team members are inspired to trust, believe in, and have faith in leaders who demonstrate the values of Kaizen in their conduct. Leaders provide an excellent example for others to follow by actively taking part in initiatives for improvement, asking for criticism, and exhibiting a willingness to learn and adapt. Moreover, executives can encourage and inspire staff members to adopt the concept and actively participate in improvement initiatives by highlighting the advantages of Kaizen through observable outcomes and success stories.

Additionally, encouraging Kaizen and uniting team members around shared goals and objectives depend on excellent communication. Leaders should make the significance of constant improvement clear, along with the goals and objectives of Kaizen projects. Leaders help staff members comprehend the importance of their contributions and how they fit with the organization's strategic objectives by giving context and justification for change. Leaders should also promote candid communication, constructive criticism, and idea exchanges to foster a transparent and cooperative culture where all individuals are encouraged to share their thoughts and feelings of worth.

Furthermore, establishing a psychologically safe atmosphere is essential to advancing Kaizen and motivating staff members to try new things, take chances, and be creative. A setting in which team members feel free to voice their thoughts, collaborate, and question the status quo without fear of criticism or retaliation is known as psychological safety. Leaders are essential in fostering an atmosphere of empathy, respect, and trust, fostering psychological safety. A supportive environment is created by leaders who exhibit humility, actively listen, and value varied viewpoints. This encourages people to venture outside their comfort zones and explore new opportunities.

It is also crucial to give staff members the tools, encouragement, and training they need to participate in Kaizen activities successfully. Leaders must invest in their workforce's skill and capability development, providing them with the necessary resources and expertise to spearhead improvement projects effectively. One way to do this is to give people access to coaching sessions, workshops, and training programs on subjects like problem-solving, root cause analysis, and Lean approaches. Leaders should also set aside time and funds for Kaizen initiatives, ensuring staff members have the time and energy to commit to improvement projects without interfering with their daily duties.

Furthermore, maintaining momentum in Kaizen projects and promoting beneficial habits depend heavily on acknowledging and celebrating successes. Whether through official recognition programs, awards, or public acknowledgment, leaders should recognize and honor people and groups for their contributions to improvement initiatives. Through acknowledging accomplishments, leaders motivate others to follow their example and emphasize the need for ongoing development. Publicly recognizing achievements also fosters a culture of Kaizen within the company by showcasing its dedication to quality and inspiring others to take an active role in improvement initiatives.

Furthermore, encouraging an accountability culture is crucial to advancing Kaizen and guaranteeing that improvement projects produce noticeable outcomes. Leaders should set precise objectives, measurements, and performance standards for improvement projects while holding individuals and groups responsible for their contributions. Leaders create a sense of urgency and accountability that propels continuous development by establishing high standards and offering frequent feedback on accomplishments. Additionally, to build resilience and perseverance in Kaizen initiatives, leaders should promote a growth mentality that sees failures as teaching opportunities and motivates people to keep going in the face of obstacles.

In addition, encouraging cooperation and teamwork is crucial to the success of Kaizen projects. It is recommended that leaders foster cross-functional collaboration and provide avenues for staff members to collaborate on improvement projects. Teams can provide creative ideas and effect significant change by combining a variety of viewpoints, abilities, and knowledge. Furthermore, to dismantle organizational silos and advance a collaborative and cooperative culture, leaders should encourage communication and knowledge exchange among team members.

In conclusion, cultivating a continuous improvement culture inside enterprises requires using leadership tactics that support Kaizen. Leaders may establish an environment conducive to the growth of Kaizen principles by setting a good example, communicating, ensuring psychological safety, offering resources and assistance, recognizing accomplishments, encouraging accountability, fostering collaboration, and empowering staff members. Leaders drive positive change and innovation throughout the organization by modeling and encouraging people to adopt the continuous improvement mindset through their actions and behaviors. In the end, realizing the full potential of Kaizen and attaining long-term success in the cutthroat corporate world of today depends on having strong leadership.

Communication and Collaboration Enhancement

Effective teamwork and organizational performance depend heavily on improving communication and collaboration. Effective communication and teamwork are critical for fostering creativity, resolving complicated issues, and accomplishing shared objectives in today's linked and hectic work environments. Organizations may build a supportive environment where people feel empowered to share ideas, offer criticism, and collaborate to achieve common goals by cultivating a culture of open communication and teamwork. This section will discuss the significance of improving communication and collaboration, essential tactics for encouraging productive communication and cooperation, and the advantages of establishing a collaborative culture inside businesses.

Effective communication and cooperation are the first and most important factors in encouraging innovation and creativity in teams and organizations. Through facilitating avenues for individuals to exchange ideas, perspectives, and insights, organizations can harness their workforce's combined creativity and wisdom to produce novel solutions, goods, and services. Furthermore, when people work together, they build on one other's ideas, question presumptions, and investigate different strategies, which can result in more creative and robust outputs. Effective communication and cooperation can also aid in the dismantling of organizational silos and promote cross-functional cooperation, empowering teams to make use of a variety of perspectives, skills, and knowledge to take on challenging tasks and advance corporate success.

Furthermore, developing trust and solid connections inside teams and organizations depends on efficient communication and teamwork. People are more inclined to trust their colleagues, communicate well, and work toward shared objectives when they feel heard, valued, and respected. Organizations can cultivate a feeling of unity and belonging among team members, resulting in increased engagement, contentment, and retention, by establishing a transparent communication and cooperation culture. Practical cooperation and communication can also help avoid miscommunications, disputes, and teamwork breakdowns, resulting in more efficient workflows, more productivity, and better results for individuals and the business.

Furthermore, effective communication and collaboration are critical to fostering organizational agility and responsiveness in today's fast-paced and continuously-evolving corporate world. Organizations can quickly adjust to shifting market conditions, customer demands, and technology improvements by cultivating open communication channels and supporting collaboration across teams and departments. Collaboration also helps firms use different viewpoints and areas of expertise to spot new opportunities, reduce risks, and address obstacles head-on, setting them up for long-term success and sustainability.

Fostering a culture of psychological safety, utilizing technology and digital tools, encouraging inclusive communication practices, and offering opportunities for training and growth are all effective ways to improve communication and cooperation. Establishing a psychologically safe culture is crucial to a setting where people may voice their opinions, challenge the status quo, and speak up without worrying about criticism or retaliation. Leaders need to foster a culture of support where people feel free to express themselves honestly and participate in the discourse and where a diversity of viewpoints is acknowledged and valued.

Furthermore, technology and digital tools can facilitate communication and cooperation in today's virtual and remote work contexts. Organizations can use various digital platforms and tools, including project management software, video conferencing, and instant messaging, to help team members communicate, collaborate, and share information in real-time. Organizations can also encourage informal communication and cooperation by utilizing social media platforms, intranet sites, and online communities. This allows workers to interact, exchange ideas, and develop relationships across corporate and geographic borders.

In addition, it is imperative to foster inclusive communication methods to guarantee that every person feels acknowledged, respected, and part of the discourse. It is essential for leaders to proactively promote diversity, equity, and inclusion in teams and organizations. They should also establish avenues for individuals with varying backgrounds and opinions to participate in the discourse. This could entail making a concerted effort to get feedback from marginalized voices, giving people a forum to express their experiences and opinions, and bringing various perspectives into the decision-making process.

Furthermore, offering opportunities for training and development can assist people in developing the teamwork and communication abilities required to thrive in today's connected and collaborative work environments. Workshops, seminars, and coaching sessions on subjects including virtual collaboration, efficient team communication, active listening, and conflict resolution can be provided by organizations. Additionally, through team-based projects, cross-functional initiatives, and cooperative problem-solving exercises, firms can allow staff members to hone and utilize their communication and cooperation abilities.

In summary, improving collaboration and communication is crucial for promoting creativity, solidifying bonds with others, and increasing organizational flexibility and responsiveness. Organizations may establish an environment where people feel empowered to share ideas, offer criticism, and collaborate towards shared objectives by cultivating a culture of open communication and teamwork. Fostering a culture of psychological safety, utilizing technology and digital tools, encouraging inclusive communication practices, and offering opportunities for training and growth are all effective ways to improve communication and cooperation. Organizations may unleash the full potential of their workforce and propel success in today's dynamic and interconnected business environment by investing in enhancing communication and collaboration.

CHAPTER IX

Problem-Solving and Innovation

Techniques for Identifying and Solving Problems

Problem-solving and identification techniques are essential abilities in both personal and professional settings. Recognizing difficulties and finding practical solutions is crucial for success and producing favorable results, whether tackling complex problems in an organization, resolving disagreements in a team, or conquering project obstacles. This section will examine several problem-solving strategies, such as brainstorming, decision-making frameworks, root cause analysis, and continuous improvement approaches.

Finding the fundamental causes of issues and creating workable solutions are two things that may be accomplished with the help of root cause analysis. To see the core cause or causes that require attention, root cause analysis is methodically looking at the variables contributing to an issue, asking "why" to unearth more severe problems, and determining the root cause or causes. Individuals and groups can create focused solutions that address the underlying issues and stop recurrence by knowing the problem's origins.

Another helpful method for coming up with ideas and fixing issues is brainstorming. Organizing a group of people to produce ideas and proposals in an unstructured, judgment-free setting is known as brainstorming. Brainstorming can aid in the discovery of novel solutions to challenging issues by fostering creativity, varied thinking, and open-mindedness. Furthermore, brainstorming sessions can promote cooperation and teamwork as participants build on one another's concepts and viewpoints to create all-encompassing solutions.

Frameworks for decision-making offer an organized method for weighing possibilities and reaching well-informed conclusions to address issues. A typical decision-making framework entails defining the problem, obtaining pertinent data, coming up with and assessing possible solutions, deciding on the best course of action, and carrying out and overseeing the chosen answer. Both individuals and teams can make well-informed decisions that successfully handle the issue by adhering to a systematic decision-making process.

Furthermore, methods for continuous improvement, like Lean Six Sigma and Kaizen, provide organized ways to recognize issues and find solutions that promote organizational excellence. Based on the ideas of constant improvement found in Japan, kaizen stresses making little, gradual adjustments to systems, procedures, and behavior in order to advance and attain perfection. Lean Six Sigma is a process improvement methodology that integrates Six Sigma and Lean manufacturing concepts to find and fix process flaws and variations in order to minimize waste, enhance quality, and boost productivity.

Moreover, the scientific method offers an organized way to solve problems through the formulation of hypotheses, execution of experiments, examination of data, and formulation of conclusions. The scientific method is beneficial when solving complicated problems that need careful analysis and empirical proof. Individuals and groups can create evidence-based solutions to challenging issues by methodically testing hypotheses, gathering information, and analyzing findings using the scientific process.

Additionally, by taking into account the connections and linkages between different components within a system, systems thinking provides an all-encompassing method of problem-solving. Analyzing a system's interactions between its various parts and the potential effects of changing one component on the system as a whole are critical components of systems thinking. Through the application of systems thinking, both individuals and groups can recognize systemic problems and create solutions that go beyond band-aid fixes to address the underlying causes of challenges.

Design thinking also provides a human-centered approach to problem-solving by emphasizing comprehension of stakeholders' and end-users needs and preferences. Design thinking entails understanding users' problems, coming up with ideas for potential solutions, testing and developing those solutions, and iterating in response to user input. Through incremental refinement and the incorporation of user feedback, design thinking can guarantee that solutions are practical, efficient, and user-centric in tackling real-world issues.

To sum up, problem-solving strategies are critical abilities needed to succeed and provide favorable results in both personal and professional settings. Individuals and teams can use various techniques to solve problems and accomplish their objectives, whether brainstorming to generate creative solutions, decision-making frameworks to make informed choices, root cause analysis to uncover underlying issues, or continuous improvement methodologies to drive organizational excellence. By applying systematic and structured problem-solving techniques and integrating varied viewpoints and approaches, people and groups can create all-encompassing resolutions that tackle the underlying causes of issues and promote improvements.

Encouraging Innovation

In today's quickly changing corporate environment, innovation is now essential to success. Globally, businesses are always looking for innovative approaches to maintain their competitive edge, set themselves apart from competitors, and satisfy the changing demands of their clientele. Though innovations are frequently associated with ground-breaking discoveries and game-changing technologies, they are also deeply ingrained in the Kaizen philosophy of continual improvement. "Continuous improvement," or "kaizen," is a Japanese methodology that stresses making tiny, gradual adjustments to products, services, and processes. Even though they first appear minor, these adjustments add up over time to provide noteworthy outcomes that promote productivity, efficiency, and creativity at all organizational levels.

The foundation of Kaizen is that each person in an organization can contribute to development. Kaizen democratizes the innovation process by enabling frontline staff to spot inefficiencies, make suggestions for improvements, and implement changes in their day-to-day work. This is in contrast to traditional top-down approaches to innovation, which mostly rely on the insights and instructions of a few people. Using a bottom-up strategy, the workforce's collective wisdom and creativity are not only tapped into but also fostered a culture of ownership and accountability, making every employee feel personally invested in the company's success. Organizations can foster a sense of empowerment and ownership among their staff members, which stimulates intrinsic motivation and encourages creativity from within, by actively including them in the change process.

Kaizen also enables workers to seek new information, abilities, and viewpoints by fostering a culture of ongoing learning and development. This emphasis on education is significant in innovation because it helps people keep up with new trends, technologies, and best practices that could spark creative thinking. Organizations can enable their workforce to innovate effectively by investing in employee development and offering training and upskilling opportunities. This approach cultivates a growth mindset that encourages experimentation, iteration, and failure-based learning. Essentially, Kaizen foster Kaizen culture of continuous learning and development, in which each failure is seen as a chance for personal growth and each accomplishment is acknowledged as a step toward greatness.

The unrelenting pursuit of perfection, or "Muda" as it is known in Japanese and translates to "waste elimination," is another fundamental tenet of Kaizen. Identifying and removing waste from processes methodically allows firms to increase efficiency, simplify operations, and free up resources. Muda includes many wastes, such as inventory, overprocessing, waiting, overproduction, faults, and needless motion. Through root cause analysis, value stream mapping, and 5S (Sort, set in order, Shine, Standardize, Sustain), Kaizen helps find hidden inefficiencies and rework procedures to maximize output. By eliminating waste, businesses build a leaner, more flexible infrastructure that can swiftly adjust to shifting consumer demands and market conditions, setting the stage for long-term innovation and expansion.

Additionally, by dismantling organizational silos and encouraging cooperation and communication across functional boundaries, Kaizen foster Kaizen culture of cooperation and teamwork. Collaboration is crucial when it comes to innovation since it brings together a variety of viewpoints, skills, and ideas that can ignite creativity and lead to ground-breaking inventions. Organizations can foster synergistic interactions and chance meetings, resulting in new ideas and solutions by encouraging people to work together across departments, functions, and hierarchies. Collaboration also promotes a sense of group ownership and accountability for invention, where success is ascribed to the combined efforts of the entire organization rather than any one person's accomplishments. Kaizen fosters a collaborative culture that breaks down conventional barriers and stimulates creativity using group effort and a common goal.

Furthermore, Kaizen promotes using technology as a catalyst for innovation, using digital tools and platforms to improve efficiency, foster teamwork, and create new opportunities. Technology is a significant force behind innovation in the modern digital age. It gives businesses access to enormous data sets, advanced analytics tools, and potent automation technologies that can transform their processes and open new revenue streams. Organizations that embrace digital transformation can drive innovation at scale, rethink their business models, and revolutionize the customer experience by leveraging the potential of cutting-edge technologies like blockchain, artificial intelligence, machine learning, and the Internet of things. Technology also allows businesses to access worldwide talent pools and get over geographical restrictions, which promotes global co-creation and collaboration. Essentially, technology catalyzes innovation, enhancing the effects of Kaizen and the rate of change in the fiercely competitive business world of today.

To sum up, Kaizen provides a framework for promoting innovation within a business. In today's fast-paced and dynamic world, Kaizen helps to create sustainable growth and competitiveness by empowering workers to reach their full potential and developing a culture of continuous improvement, learning, waste reduction, collaboration, and technology adoption. Additionally, Kaizen pushes Kaizen to adopt open innovation strategies and external collaborations that capitalize on the resources and combined knowledge of external stakeholders, such as suppliers, peers in the industry, and customers. In the end, companies may establish an innovative culture that stimulates invention, encourages teamwork, and promotes continuous improvement by adopting the ideas and practices of Kaizen. This Kaizen them up for long-term success in a constantly shifting business environment.

Sustaining Long-Term Improvements

As they say, sustainability is the key to success in any undertaking, and improvement programs are no exception. Realizing long-term effects and attaining durable success requires the capacity to sustain long-term advances, whether in personal development, organizational reform, or social advancement. However, maintaining gains is frequently easier said than done because it calls for overcoming several difficulties and roadblocks that could impede advancement. To thoroughly grasp this crucial component of success, we will examine the primary ideas, tactics, and best practices for maintaining long-term progress in this section. We will do this by incorporating insights from various disciplines and domains.

The Japanese concept of Kaizen, which embodies the idea of constant development, is fundamental to maintaining long-term gains. Kaizen, which means "continuous improvement," stresses making tiny, gradual improvements to pursue excellence relentlessly. Kaizen promotes a persistent and systematic approach to improvement that gets embedded in the corporate culture, in contrast to traditional techniques that concentrate on irregular spurts of improvement followed by periods of stagnation. Organizations can establish a self-reinforcing cycle of growth and success by fostering a continuous improvement mindset, wherein minor victories generate momentum and stimulate additional innovation.

Furthermore, Kaizen promotes resilience and adaptation in the face of difficulty by encouraging firms to view failure as a teaching opportunity rather than a setback. Essentially, Kaizen fosters an unrelenting pursuit of excellence and ongoing learning, which offers a strong foundation for maintaining long-term improvements.

Alignment with the objectives and values of the organization is another essential component for maintaining long-term progress. The long-term sustainability of improvements outside the organization's larger strategic objectives is doubtful. As a result, it is crucial to guarantee that improvement projects are intimately related to the company's goal, vision, and vital values. Leaders instill a feeling of purpose and direction in their workforce by coordinating improvements with company goals, encouraging them to stick with the change initiative. Alignment also makes it easier to set priorities and distribute resources, guaranteeing that the tools and support needed to maintain gains over time are available. Furthermore, alignment promotes coherence and consistency throughout various departments and functions, averting progress undermined by competing agendas and contradictory priorities. This is how alignment ensures that efforts are concentrated and directed toward accomplishing strategic objectives as a guiding principle for maintaining long-term progress.

In addition, maintaining long-term gains necessitates a robust infrastructure and support network that permits ongoing observation, assessment, and optimization of improvement projects. This infrastructure consists of several components: accountability, feedback, and performance assessment systems. Systems for measuring performance offer the information and metrics needed to evaluate the effects of improvement projects and monitor advancement toward predetermined objectives. Establishing unambiguous performance indicators and benchmarks enables firms to track the efficacy of their improvement initiatives and pinpoint opportunities for additional optimization. Furthermore, feedback methods facilitate learning and adaptation by allowing stakeholders to offer suggestions and insights into the improvement process. Asking staff members, clients, and other stakeholders for their opinions—through surveys, focus groups, or routine check-ins—ensures that improvement projects are adaptable to the needs and conditions that change over time. Furthermore, accountability methods ensure that progress is not halted by complacency or indifference by holding individuals and teams accountable for their roles and responsibilities in maintaining improvements. Organizations foster an accountability culture by clearly defining responsibilities, expectations, and rewards, strengthening the commitment to maintaining long-term gains.

Effective change management and leadership are necessary for maintaining long-term improvements, in addition to infrastructure and support systems. The framework and resources offered by change management help people and organizations navigate the change process and guarantee the successful and seamless implementation of improvements. Implementing change management techniques, like communication plans, stakeholder engagement tactics, or training programs, can reduce resistance and promote the acceptance of new habits. In addition, change management cultivates an agile and resilient culture that helps firms adjust to shifting conditions and maintain gains over time. Similarly, leadership is essential to maintaining long-term gains giving workers motivation, guidance, and vision. Proficient leaders explain the reasoning behind modifications, unite interested parties around common objectives, and enable staff members to take charge of enhancement initiatives. Leaders establish a culture of responsibility, trust, and cooperation that maintains momentum and encourages creativity by setting an example of desirable behaviors and values. Moreover, by coaching, mentoring, or removing barriers, leadership offers the tools and resources required for staff members to flourish. Put leadership and change management facilitate long-term improvements by providing the direction, encouragement, and support needed to overcome change's challenges.

Furthermore, a culture of learning and adaptability that promotes experimentation, creativity, and constant development is necessary to maintain long-term gains. Businesses that adopt a growth mentality are more adaptable and resilient, ready to take advantage of new possibilities and adjust to changing conditions. Organizations may establish a setting where people are inspired to try new things, take measured chances, and learn from successes and failures by cultivating a learning culture. Additionally, firms that make learning and development investments can better adapt to new obstacles and changes, guaranteeing that advancements continue to be applicable and valuable. A learning culture also helps companies use their employees' combined creativity and intelligence, drawing from various viewpoints and experiences that stimulate creativity and problem-solving. Organizations that put learning first gain a long-lasting competitive edge that helps them prosper in today's fast-paced, dynamic business world, whether through formal training programs, knowledge-sharing initiatives, or communities of practice.

Furthermore, maintaining long-term gains necessitates a dedication to ongoing innovation and reinvention, which helps businesses stay ahead of the curve and foresee problems and trends in the future. In the current dynamic business environment, companies that take their success for granted are swiftly surpassed by more adaptable and creative rivals. As a result, promoting an innovative culture that values cooperation, experimentation, and creativity is crucial. Organizations can empower their employees to explore novel concepts, question established practices, and seek ground-breaking solutions by offering the resources and support needed for innovation. Additionally, companies that use open innovation strategies—like collaborations, co-creation, and crowdsourcing—are better able to tap into outside knowledge and perspectives that spur innovation and value creation. Moreover, companies investing in technology adoption and research and development (R&D) are better positioned to take advantage of new opportunities and adapt to changing client demands. Organizations that prioritize innovation have a sustained competitive edge that helps them adjust and prosper in today's fast-paced and uncertain business climate, whether through process, product, or business model innovation.

To sum up, maintaining long-term gains necessitates a comprehensive strategy that takes into account several factors, such as ongoing development, alignment with the organization's objectives and core values, infrastructure and support systems, change management and leadership, a culture of learning and adaptation, and a dedication to ongoing innovation and reinvention. Organizations can establish a competitive and sustainable culture of excellence by incorporating these components into their corporate DNA. Furthermore, maintaining long-term gains necessitates adopting a long-term viewpoint that views change as a process rather than an endpoint. Organizations may successfully negotiate the challenges of today's business environment and become stronger, more resilient, and more innovative than ever by staying agile, adaptable, and forward-thinking. In the end, maintaining long-term improvements involves more than just making short-term gains; it also entails laying the groundwork for long-term success and prosperity that benefits society, shareholders, consumers, and employees.

CHAPTER X

Common Obstacles and How to Overcome Them

Identifying Common Barriers to Continuous Improvement

In personal and corporate contexts, continuous improvement is a critical concept that promotes continuing process, system, and behavior refinement. Despite its significance, the road to ongoing improvement is frequently paved with roadblocks that can prevent advancement. To successfully navigate and overcome these typical obstacles, one must recognize and comprehend them. This section examines some of the most common barriers to ongoing development and explains their emergence and solutions.

Resistance to change is one of the main obstacles to ongoing improvement. Individuals have an innate tendency to adhere to well-known routines and procedures, and any change from the norm may be viewed as dangerous. This resistance is frequently caused by a lack of trust in the novel approaches being offered, a fear of the unknown, and uncertainty about the results of change. Workers may fear losing their jobs, have trouble adjusting to new working practices, or have doubts about the advantages that continuous improvement programs claim to offer. Effective change management techniques are needed to overcome this obstacle, such as providing employees with training and support to acquire new skills, communicating the benefits of the change clearly and understandably, and integrating staff members in the change process to make them feel important and heard.

Lack of leadership and a clear vision is another major obstacle. Leaders with a strong vision and dedication to the process are necessary for continuous improvement to get traction and thrive. Lackluster, inconsistent, or non-visible leadership fosters a confused and unsupportive atmosphere. Workers must observe their leaders exhibiting the attitudes and actions linked to ongoing development. Leaders should express the vision often, establish specific objectives, and acknowledge and celebrate modest victories to keep things moving forward. Efforts to improve continually can quickly become sidetracked and falter without solid leadership.

Lack of resources is a third obstacle. Initiatives for continuous improvement frequently call for investing financial, human, and temporal resources. Companies may be hesitant to commit these resources, particularly if the advantages take time to materialize. This may result in a haphazard implementation, with teams needing more resources, expertise, or time to pursue improvement initiatives. Making a solid business case for continuous improvement is crucial to overcoming this obstacle. This can be done by using case studies, pilot projects, and thorough plans that specify the costs and benefits of the improvement. These efforts will only be successful if executive sponsorship is obtained and teams are provided with the necessary resources.

Lack of involvement and engagement from employees is another frequent obstacle. Environments where workers at all levels actively participate in and take responsibility for the improvement process are ideal for continuous improvement. However, staff members might not feel connected to these projects at many companies because they aren't involved in decision-making or need to understand how their efforts matter. Poor communication, a lack of acknowledgment, and opportunities for staff members to provide ideas and comments can all worsen this disengagement. Organizations should create an inclusive, collaborative culture where workers are valued for their contributions and encouraged to share their ideas to increase employee engagement. Recurring feedback loops and unobstructed communication channels are vital for preserving elevated levels of employee engagement and guaranteeing that their opinions are acknowledged and appreciated.

The absence of a systematic strategy to progress is the sixth obstacle. Continuous improvement is a process that takes place over time and calls for a disciplined and organized approach. Businesses that don't have a defined improvement process or framework frequently find it challenging to maintain momentum and produce significant outcomes. With a systematic approach, work may become consistent and dispersed, which can cause dissatisfaction and burnout. Organizations should use proven continuous improvement techniques, like Lean, Six Sigma, or the Plan-Do-Check-Act (PDCA) cycle, to get over this obstacle. By offering an organized method for finding, putting into practice, and maintaining changes, these frameworks ensure that initiatives are targeted, cohesive, and aligned with company objectives.

The existence of organizational silos is another obstacle. Within many organizations, various teams or departments function independently from one another and seldom communicate or work together. These silos can impede ongoing progress by obstructing the exchange of ideas and information. It is challenging to recognize and resolve cross-functional problems when teams don't collaborate or share expertise, which results in mediocre fixes and lost chances for advancement. To dismantle these silos, it is necessary to promote a transparent and collaborative culture where teams are motivated to exchange information, cooperate on projects for improvement, and see their job as a component of a more considerable organizational structure. Regular interdepartmental meetings and cross-functional teams can aid in bridging gaps and advancing a more integrated approach to continuous development.

A notable obstacle is the need for more information and measurements to monitor advancement. Data plays a critical role in continuous improvement by helping to pinpoint problem areas, assess the effects of improvements, and guide decisions. Organizations can only evaluate their performance or the success of their improvement initiatives with accurate data and relevant indicators. As a result, judgments may be made based more on conjecture than on solid data, wasting money and producing subpar results. Organizations should set up reliable data collection and analysis procedures to overcome this obstacle and guarantee timely and correct information access. In order to support continuous improvement initiatives, key performance indicators (KPIs) and other metrics need to be precisely established, routinely checked, and utilized.

Cultural inertia, which occurs when ingrained organizational culture opposes novel methods of thinking and doing, is another obstacle. This resistance can take many forms, including cynicism against novel approaches, resistance to embracing new technologies, or devotion to antiquated customs. It takes a deliberate effort to change the organizational mindset and promote a culture that values and supports continuous improvement in order to overcome cultural inertia. This can be accomplished via activities that show the advantages of change, leadership commitment, and continual education and training. Building momentum and progressively changing the company culture can also be achieved by acknowledging people and groups that exhibit the desired behaviors and celebrating little victories.

Lastly, fear of failing can be a significant obstacle to ongoing development. Failure is stigmatized in many organizations, which makes people risk-averse and reluctant to try out novel concepts. This anxiety can inhibit creativity and discourage companies from pursuing potentially game-changing advancements. Organizations should foster a culture that sees failure as a chance for learning and development rather than as a setback in order to overcome this obstacle. One way to lessen the fear of failure and foster a more creative and resilient company is to support experimentation, create a safe space for taking chances, and prioritize learning objectives over punitive actions.

In conclusion, attaining sustainable development and growth requires recognizing and removing frequent obstacles to ongoing improvement. Significant barriers that can obstruct efforts at continuous improvement include organizational silos, fear of failure, lack of data and metrics, lack of clear leadership and vision, employee disengagement, organizational resistance to change, and insufficient resources. Organizations can foster a continuous improvement environment that promotes and maintains improved performance, innovation, and success by recognizing these obstacles and implementing measures to address them.

Strategies to Overcome Resistance and Setbacks

Getting beyond obstacles and opposition is a crucial task for any business looking to make improvements or adjustments. There are many different reasons why people resist change, such as contentment with the status quo, lack of understanding, fear of the unknown, and loss of control. Setbacks can be brought about by unanticipated difficulties, a lack of resources, or early mistakes. In order to effectively tackle these obstacles, organizations need to implement efficacious tactics that target the underlying reasons for resistance and convert setbacks into chances for development and education.

Clear and persistent communication is one of the best tactics for getting beyond opposition. Leaders must convey to all stakeholders the change's vision, purpose, and advantages in a clear and consistent manner when putting it into practice. By providing an answer to the crucial question of "why" the change is required, this promotes comprehension and buy-in. Transparent communication provides a clear roadmap of what to expect, how it will affect individuals, and the overall goals, which lowers uncertainty and fear. Frequent updates on developments and benchmarks support involvement and show that the transition is being handled skillfully.

Including stakeholders early on in the process of transformation is another important tactic. Participating in planning and decision-making processes with staff members, particularly those who will be directly impacted by the change, increases a sense of ownership and decreases resistance. People are more likely to support the change when they believe that their worries and opinions are valued. Proactive problem-solving is made possible by the collaborative approach's ability to identify possible problems early on. Establishing change advocates—powerful people who can speak up for the change—inside the organization can also aid in creating momentum and support from within the ranks.

Overcoming opposition to change requires both education and training. Giving staff members the abilities and information they need to adjust to new procedures or systems lowers tension and boosts self-assurance. Training curricula must to be customized to meet the unique requirements and gaps found in the workforce. Apart from official training, employees can benefit from continuous assistance like coaching, mentorship, and resource access, which can strengthen their learning and act as a safety net while they adjust to the shift.

Overcoming resistance in an organization requires first establishing trust. Consistent behaviors that exhibit dependability, honesty, and respect foster trust. By being open and honest about the difficulties and unknowns that come with the shift, owning up to mistakes, and accepting accountability for problems, leaders can foster trust. Employees are more inclined to support a change project even in the face of challenges if they believe that their leaders are really concerned about their well-being and are committed to its success.

It's also critical to address the emotional aspects of transformation. Anxiety, uncertainty, and a sense of loss are common reactions to change. In order to help staff members handle these feelings, leaders must acknowledge them and offer support. This can be accomplished through stress management initiatives, counseling services, and public forums where staff members can voice their worries. Resistance can be greatly decreased by fostering a supportive workplace where workers feel free to express their worries and frustrations without worrying about repercussions.

Adaptability and flexibility are essential tactics for handling obstacles during the transition process. Unexpected challenges frequently arise during change initiatives, necessitating alterations to the initial strategy. Leaders need to have the flexibility and problem-solving mentality to change course and adjust tactics as necessary. This could entail shifting priorities, altering schedules, or reassessing objectives. Being flexible makes it possible for the company to adapt quickly to changing conditions and turn possible setbacks into chances for innovation and growth.

Celebrating accomplishments, no matter how minor, is another powerful tactic for getting over obstacles and disappointments. Acknowledging and applauding any advancement, no matter how tiny, boosts spirits and momentum. It reaffirms the idea that the reform project is headed in the correct path and that the efforts are paying off. There are many different ways to celebrate, from official award programs to casual get-togethers with the team. Leaders may maintain employee motivation and goal focus by emphasizing accomplishments.

Reducing opposition can also be aided by outlining the benefits of the change in plain and concrete terms. Employees are more inclined to accept a change if they can directly benefit from it in their personal or professional lives. The precise benefits of the change, such as increased productivity, better working conditions, or chances for professional advancement, should be communicated by leaders. Making a strong case for support can involve demonstrating how the change is in line with both individual and corporate objectives.

Lastly, overcoming obstacles and failures requires keeping an eye on the big picture. The process of change requires patience and perseverance. Leaders need to be persistent and patient, understanding that obstacles are an inevitable part of the process of change. It's critical to maintain your attention on the big picture and to resist giving up on short-term difficulties. Constant observation and assessment of the change process can yield insightful information and support in making the required corrections to stay on course.

In summary, overcoming opposition and obstacles necessitates a multimodal strategy that takes into account both the pragmatic and affective facets of transformation. Critical techniques for managing the complexity of change include open and constant communication, stakeholder involvement, education and training, fostering trust, handling emotions, adaptability, acknowledging successes, emphasizing advantages, and keeping an eye on the big picture. By using these techniques, leaders may lessen resistance, deal with failures skillfully, and spearhead change projects that result in long-term development and progress.

Real-life Examples and Solutions

Examples of continuous improvement from the natural world and the solutions resulting from this concept offer essential insights into how little adjustments over time can significantly impact. The Japanese concept of Kaizen, which is the foundation of the continuous improvement approach, stresses making gradual, constructive improvements that add to significant gains over time. This section examines actual cases from various industries, including manufacturing, healthcare, personal growth, and business settings, demonstrating the practical application of the Kaizen approach and the solutions it has generated.

Toyota is frequently cited as the epitome of the Kaizen principle in action in the industrial industry. Kaizen is a critical component of the Toyota Production System (TPS), which has significantly increased output and quality. One noteworthy example is the company's policy of permitting assembly line workers to halt production if they discover a flaw. This approach, sometimes referred to as "jidoka" or automation with a human touch, allows staff members to spot problems immediately and take immediate action to fix them, stopping the manufacturing line from moving on with defective goods. This has dramatically decreased waste and raised the caliber of the products over time. This practice's continual feedback loop promotes ongoing attention to detail and small-step advancements, demonstrating how minor adjustments may significantly impact an organization.

Another instance in the manufacturing sector is Motorola, which implemented Six Sigma concepts, a system similar to Kaizen. Motorola was able to dramatically increase the quality of its products and the satisfaction of its customers by concentrating on making process improvements and process reductions. For instance, in their mobile phone division, constant observation and small-step process enhancements resulted in a significant drop in defect rates, which raised reliability and satisfied customers. This dedication to ongoing development strengthened Motorola's market competitiveness and improved its products' quality.

Implementing Kaizen concepts in the healthcare industry has resulted in notable enhancements to operational efficiency and patient care. Seattle, Washington's Virginia Mason Medical Center offers an interesting case study. Virginia Mason created the Virginia Mason Production System (VMPS) by implementing the Toyota Production System and extending its ideas to the healthcare industry. This strategy is centered on improving patient care, reducing waste, and simplifying procedures. The decrease in patient wait times was one of the main results of VMPS. By implementing minor adjustments like streamlining patient flow, harmonizing protocols, and empowering employees to recognize and resolve issues, the medical facility significantly decreased wait times, raised patient contentment, and increased overall effectiveness. The success of Virginia Mason serves as an example of how Kaizen can be successfully applied to various industries to promote better results and ongoing improvement.

The concepts of Kaizen have been successfully applied to habit formation and personal development in personal development. Deeply exploring this idea, James Clear's book "Atomic Habits" highlights the ability of little, regular acts to create enduring habits. Precise offers a plethora of real-life instances of people who have changed their lives by making minor, gradual adjustments. The tale of the man who began by performing only one push-up each day serves as one illustration. He steadily developed a habit of regular exercise by concentrating on this tiny, doable action, which ultimately resulted in notable health gains.

This strategy emphasizes the core of Kaizen, which is to make minor adjustments to produce remarkable, long-term effects continuously. The "Atomic Habits" success stories attest to the Kaizen mindset's efficacy in fostering human growth.

Corporate settings are also excellent places to observe the effects of Kaizen. Atlassian's software development business has promoted a culture of innovation and continual improvement by applying Kaizen concepts. Employees at Atlassian are encouraged to dedicate 20% of their work hours to initiatives that pique their interest. This approach has resulted in the creation of several cutting-edge products and solutions. Known as "Ship It Days," this procedure enables staff members to pinpoint problem areas, try out fresh concepts, and gradually apply adjustments. Creating "JIRA," a viral project management tool now a mainstay of the business's product line, was one noteworthy result. By cultivating a culture that prioritizes employee contributions and continual improvement, Atlassian has managed to sustain its competitive advantage in the software business while propelling innovation.

A multinational corporation, Walmart has implemented Kaizen principles in the retail industry to improve customer service and streamline processes. "Kaizen blitzes," or Kaizen events, are a technique used by Walmart's distribution hubs to find inefficiencies and make tiny, gradual changes. One distribution center, for example, concentrated on shortening the time it took for trucks to be unloaded. The center drastically reduced unloading times, boosted productivity, and increased efficiency by implementing minor adjustments, such as restructuring the unloading procedure and streamlining the warehouse structure. Kaizen events cultivate a culture of ongoing enhancement and staff involvement, resulting in long-term operational excellence.

Kaizen ideas have been used in education to improve student results and instructional strategies. The Chugach School District in Alaska changed its approach to teaching via a dedication to ongoing improvement. The district engaged teachers, students, and the community by identifying improvement areas. These efforts resulted in a number of small changes that, over time, led to considerable improvements in student engagement and performance. The modifications included personalized learning programs, ongoing evaluation, and frequent feedback loops. Higher graduation rates and better student accomplishment were the outcomes of this cooperative strategy, which promoted a culture of continual improvement.

Another sector that offers instances of Kaizen in action is the hotel sector. The Ritz-Carlton Hotel Company has been renowned for its dedication to quality and client pleasure for many years. The organization empowers its staff to find and apply minor enhancements in service delivery by implementing Kaizen concepts. Front-line employees are, for instance, urged to document and resolve any problems or areas for development they come across in their everyday dealings with visitors. The company's reputation for providing excellent customer experience has been enhanced by its proactive attitude, resulting in various guest service advancements. The success of The Ritz-Carlton shows how a dedication to ongoing development can result in excellent customer service and devoted patronage.

Kaizen's ideas have been used for environmental sustainability to improve sustainability processes and minimize waste. For example, a large corporation, Unilever, used Kaizen to reduce its environmental impact. Unilever has made notable progress in mitigating its ecological footprint by gradually modifying its manufacturing procedures, packaging, and waste management practices. The company's environmental objectives have been aided by initiatives including boosting the use of recyclable materials, cutting energy consumption, and optimizing water usage. Unilever is a prime example of how Kaizen can promote corporate responsibility and environmental sustainability through continuous improvement.

Finally, real-world instances of Kaizen applications in various industries demonstrate the significant influence of ongoing development. The Kaizen ideology promotes a culture of gradual change, employee participation, and data-driven decision-making in a variety of industries, including manufacturing, healthcare, personal development, corporate environments, retail, education, hospitality, and environmental sustainability. These illustrations highlight Kaizen's adaptability and success in bringing about notable and long-lasting improvements. Organizations and individuals can achieve long-term success and fulfillment by adopting the Kaizen attitude, improving efficiency, and encouraging creativity.

CHAPTER XI

Measuring Progress and Success

Tools and Metrics for Tracking Improvements

Any business that wants to track changes must use metrics and tools designed to assess results, gauge progress, and ensure that objectives are being successfully accomplished. By implementing these tools and metrics, continuous improvement can be approached organized, enabling data-driven decision-making and promoting an open and accountable culture. This section will examine the several metrics and technologies available to businesses for tracking changes, emphasizing their value, capabilities, and advantages for promoting long-term advancement.

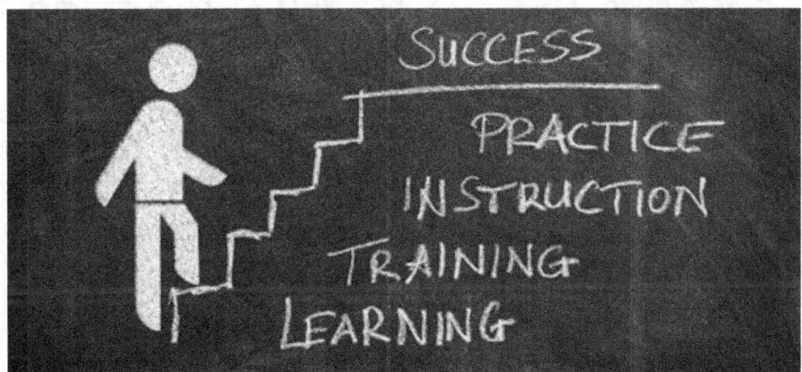

The Balanced Scorecard is one of the most used instruments for monitoring progress (BSC). The Balanced Scorecard, created by David Norton and Robert Kaplan, offers a thorough framework for converting an organization's strategic goals into performance metrics from four angles: learning and growth, internal business processes, customers, and finances. With the help of this tool, businesses can keep an eye on their performance from various perspectives, resulting in a well-rounded improvement strategy. The customer perspective gauges customer satisfaction and retention; the internal business processes perspective assesses the efficacy and efficiency of internal operations; the learning and growth perspective evaluates the organization's capacity for innovation and the development of its human capital. The financial perspective concentrates on profitability and cost management. Organizations can use the Balanced Scorecard to monitor their progress, make well-informed decisions to promote continuous improvement and match their daily operations with their strategic objectives.

The Key Performance Indicator is another valuable tool for monitoring progress (KPI). Key Performance Indicators (KPIs) are precise, measurable metrics that businesses use to assess how well they accomplish essential goals. Depending on the sector and the company's particular objectives, these metrics can differ significantly. While a customer service firm could concentrate on customer satisfaction scores, response times, and resolution rates, a manufacturing company might monitor KPIs linked to production efficiency, defect rates, and on-time delivery. KPIs offer a precise and impartial method for assessing performance, pinpointing areas needing development, and monitoring advancement over time. Establishing unambiguous objectives and periodically analyzing KPI data allows firms to stay on course and modify to meet their goals.

The Plan-Do-Check-Act (PDCA) cycle is another crucial instrument for monitoring progress. The PDCA cycle, sometimes called the Deming Cycle, is an organized, iterative method for problem-solving and ongoing development. Plan, Do, Check, and Act are the cycle's four phases. Organizations identify an issue or area for improvement, define goals, and create a strategy to address it during the planning stage. They test the plan's efficacy by putting it into practice on a modest scale during the Do stage. During the Check phase, they monitor and assess the outcomes to see if the plan produces the expected results. Lastly, if the plan is successful, they make any required modifications and carry it out more broadly in the Act stage. The PDCA cycle encourages a systematic improvement approach, ensuring that changes are thoroughly planned, tested, and refined before being fully adopted.

Benchmarking is yet another crucial instrument for monitoring advancements. Benchmarking is evaluating an organization's performance in relation to industry norms or best practices to pinpoint areas for improvement. This procedure can be carried out publicly by assessing the company against rivals or leaders in the sector or internally by comparing various teams or departments inside the company. Benchmarking helps uncover areas for development and provides insightful information about how well the company is doing compared to others. Establishing benchmarks and periodically evaluating performance against them allows companies to monitor their advancement and work toward meeting or surpassing industry norms.

Lean Six Sigma is an approach that aims to drive waste elimination and continuous improvement by combining the ideas of Six Sigma and Lean manufacturing. Lean emphasizes adding customer value by eliminating non-value-added tasks, whereas Six Sigma seeks to lower process variability and errors. Lean Six Sigma, when combined, offers a potent framework for monitoring advancements and reaching operational perfection. Organizations may monitor process performance, identify inefficiencies, and evaluate data by utilizing a variety of Lean Six Sigma framework tools, including Root Cause Analysis (RCA), Value Stream Mapping (VSM), and Control Charts. Value Stream Mapping is helpful for firms to map their workflows, find waste, and create more effective procedures. Organizations can more effectively handle issues by determining the underlying causes of problems using root cause analysis. Control charts give businesses a visual depiction of the performance of their processes over time, enabling them to monitor stability and spot any patterns or deviations that need to be taken seriously. Organizations can methodically track changes, save waste, and improve quality using Lean Six Sigma techniques.

Dashboards are a useful additional tool for monitoring progress. Dashboards are graphic representations of essential performance indicators offering real-time data and insights. With these technologies, businesses can keep tabs on target progress, evaluate performance quickly, and make informed decisions based on facts. Numerous data, including sales success, customer satisfaction, operational effectiveness, and financial health, can be configured to appear on dashboards. Dashboards give organizations a centralized view of performance data, enabling them to stay informed, spot opportunities for development, and respond quickly to problems. Dashboards ensure that all stakeholders have access to the data required to drive continuous improvement, promoting transparency and accountability.

Organizations can track changes using a variety of metrics in addition to these methods. The Return on Investment (ROI), which gauges the financial return an investment or project generates compared to its cost, is one popular indicator. ROI assists businesses in determining the success of their improvement projects and allocating resources wisely. The Net Promoter Score (NPS), which gauges client pleasure and loyalty, is another crucial indicator. Customers' likelihood of recommending the company's goods or services to others is surveyed, and the answers are divided into three categories: promoters, passives, and detractors. This process yields the net promoter score (NPS). Organizations can measure customer satisfaction, pinpoint areas for development, and implement remedial measures to improve the customer experience by monitoring Net Promoter Score.

Another crucial indicator for monitoring progress is employee engagement. Better organizational success, reduced employee attrition, and higher productivity correlate with high levels of employee engagement. Employers can gauge worker involvement with surveys, feedback systems, and other evaluation instruments. Organizations can pinpoint areas where their management style, staff development initiatives, or workplace culture need improvement by routinely evaluating engagement levels. This fosters a more dedicated and driven workforce, which is necessary to promote ongoing improvement.

Process efficiency, which gauges how well a company uses its resources to generate goods or services, is another important statistic. Numerous metrics, including cycle time, lead time, and throughput, can be used to measure this. Cycle time is needed to finish a process from beginning to end, whereas lead time is required to start and see it through. The quantity of goods produced or services provided in a specific time is measured by throughput. Organizations can increase productivity and efficiency by reducing waste, identifying bottlenecks, and optimizing operations.

Tracking advancements also requires the use of quality metrics. These measures, which may include customer complaints, defect rates, and error rates, evaluate the quality of goods or services the company provides. Organizations can fulfill industry standards and consumer expectations by monitoring quality measurements by identifying areas for process, product, or service improvement. Establishing quality control procedures, such as testing, audits, and inspections, can assist businesses in upholding high standards and promoting ongoing development.

Lastly, innovation metrics are essential for monitoring advancements in a company's capacity for innovation and adaptation to shifting market dynamics. These indicators can include the number of new goods or services created, the time it takes to introduce them to the market, and the share of sales from new goods or services. Organizations can evaluate their ability to innovate, pinpoint areas where R&D expenditures are required, and promote a culture of experimentation and creativity by monitoring innovation metrics. Innovation measurement and encouragement promote long-term performance and competitiveness by keeping businesses adaptable to changing market conditions and client demands.

In conclusion, using various tools and metrics that offer information about an organization's performance, advancement, and opportunities for development is necessary for tracking improvements. Performance can be measured and tracked in an organized way with the help of tools like dashboards, Lean Six Sigma, benchmarking, PDCA cycles, Key Performance Indicators, and Balanced Scorecards. Metrics that provide particular indications of success and opportunities for improvement include ROI, NPS, employee engagement, process efficiency, quality, and innovation. Organizations can achieve sustainable development and success, generate continuous improvement, and make data-driven decisions using these tools and measurements.

Celebrating Small Wins and Milestones

Honoring minor victories and achievements is a crucial habit that can significantly influence people's drive, spirits, and well-being. Even though significant accomplishments and turning points are frequently celebrated with fanfare and enthusiasm, it is equally critical to recognize and honor the smaller wins and advancements made along the way. This section will discuss the value of acknowledging little victories and accomplishments, its advantages for people and businesses, and practical ways to apply this habit to day-to-day activities.

Fundamentally, praising little victories and accomplishments is about appreciating growth—no matter how small—and the hard work and commitment needed to get there. Every minor victory is worth celebrating, whether finishing a task ahead of schedule, accomplishing a personal objective, or conquering a problematic situation. P pausing to consider these accomplishments can reinforce positive habits, increase their self-esteem, and maintain their motivation to continue. Additionally, since each accomplishment is a stepping stone to the next, celebrating modest victories encourages people to keep moving forward and achieve more significant objectives.

In addition, acknowledging minor victories and accomplishments promotes a culture of gratitude and acknowledgment in businesses. There's a sense of unity, belonging, and purpose when team leaders and peers take the time to recognize and congratulate their members' accomplishments. Workers are more engaged, loyal, and committed to the company when they feel their contributions are respected and appreciated. Additionally, as team members witness the results of their combined efforts and encourage one another to reach common objectives, celebrating little victories fosters trust and teamwork.

In addition, acknowledging little victories and life achievements helps to foster a positive attitude toward the world. Taking the time to recognize and appreciate tiny triumphs serves as a reminder that growth is a journey rather than a destination in a world where success is frequently associated with significant accomplishments and rapid pleasure. People can learn to be resilient, grateful, and optimistic even in the face of adversity by concentrating on the positive parts of their lives and appreciating their progress. In the long run, having a positive outlook makes people more resilient and adaptable since it benefits their mental and emotional health and increases their capacity to handle obstacles and disappointments.

Furthermore, acknowledging little victories and accomplishments keeps people inspired and dedicated to their objectives. When people see concrete proof of their advancements and successes, it boosts their self-confidence and encourages them to keep going in the face of challenges or disappointments. Larger objectives can be broken down into smaller, more achievable benchmarks so that people can more easily monitor their progress and recognize each tiny victory. This sense of accomplishment bolsters Their motivation and resolve, which moves them one step closer to their ultimate goals.

Furthermore, acknowledging and appreciating minor victories and achievements makes people feel happy and fulfilled. People feel happier, prouder of themselves, and more fulfilled when they take the time to recognize and appreciate their accomplishments, no matter how minor. This improves their general well-being. This happy emotional state benefits people's relationships, productivity, general quality of life, and physical and mental health. People can develop a stronger sense of contentment, satisfaction, and purpose by making it a habit to celebrate little victories. This will result in a life that is more meaningful and fulfilling.

In addition, acknowledging modest victories and accomplishments encourages originality and inventiveness in businesses. Employees are more willing to take chances, think creatively, and try out novel concepts and methods when they feel valued and acknowledged for their contributions. Organizations can remain flexible and adaptable in a business environment that is changing quickly thanks to this innovative and experimental culture, which boosts competitiveness and growth. Furthermore, acknowledging minor victories encourages staff members to push the envelope of what is feasible since they can personally witness the results of their work and gain motivation to reach higher, more challenging objectives.

In conclusion, acknowledging little victories and accomplishments is an effective habit that can significantly improve people's lives and the performance of businesses. Acknowledging and valuing the incremental gains made along the journey can help people feel more confident, motivated, and better about themselves. Furthermore, recognizing and celebrating little victories encourages an environment of gratitude, cooperation, and recognition, increasing productivity, employee engagement, and loyalty. Furthermore, recognizing little victories encourages resilience, happiness, and creativity by promoting a positive attitude in life. In the end, people and organizations may build a culture of success, fulfillment, and continual growth that helps them get closer to their objectives by celebrating minor victories in their everyday lives and work.

Adapting and Evolving Your Kaizen Practices

In today's dynamic and rapidly shifting business world, organizations that want to promote continuous improvement and achieve sustained success must adapt and evolve their Kaizen processes. Kaizen, a Japanese continuous improvement philosophy, stresses making little, gradual adjustments to systems, procedures, and behaviors to advance and attain perfection. Although the ideas of Kaizen are ageless, organizations need to modify and advance their Kaizen methods to stay current and efficient in the face of changing opportunities, trends, and problems. The significance of modifying and developing Kaizen techniques, the main forces behind change in the contemporary business environment, and workable tactics for staying ahead of the curve and promoting continuous improvement will all be covered in this section.

The need to adjust and develop Kaizen methods stems from maintaining an organization's flexibility, resilience, and responsiveness to dynamic market circumstances and creating patterns. Organizations encounter a wide range of issues in today's quickly evolving business environment, such as global rivalry, increasing consumer preferences, and technology disruption. Organizations must respond swiftly and effectively to new possibilities and challenges to survive in this dynamic environment. Organizations can maintain a competitive edge and promote long-term growth by adapting their Kaizen methods to recognize new trends better, foresee needs, and proactively handle possible risks.

Furthermore, utilizing innovation and creativity within enterprises requires adjusting and developing Kaizen methods. Any successful business depends on innovation to drive competitive advantage, process optimization, and product development. However, creativity and revolutionary change may not necessarily be fueled by the incremental improvements that are the main focus of traditional Kaizen approaches. Organizations can cultivate an innovative culture and seize fresh chances for expansion and distinction by modifying and advancing Kaizen processes to include aspects of design thinking, creativity, and experimentation. Organizations may also push the envelope and create revolutionary change by embracing innovation and risk-taking. This helps them stay ahead of the competition and achieve long-term success.

Additionally, encouraging employee involvement, empowerment, and ownership requires modifying and improving Kaizen processes. Attaining company goals and promoting continuous development depend heavily on employee involvement. On the other hand, employees' sense of empowerment and ownership may be fostered by something other than conventional top-down methods of Kaizen. Organizations can foster a culture where employees feel appreciated, respected, and empowered to offer their ideas, insights, and skills for continuous improvement by extending Kaizen's methods to lean leadership, servant leadership, and employee empowerment principles. Organizations can also give staff members the tools to effect positive change and realize their full potential by offering training, development, and growth opportunities.

Kaizen procedures must also be updated if new technologies and digital tools are used to promote continuous improvement. Organizations can analyze success, spur innovation, and find areas for improvement with the abundance of data, analytics, and technological solutions available in the modern digital age. Organizations can obtain more profound insights into their operations, spot patterns, and trends, and make data-driven decisions to promote continuous improvement by incorporating digital tools like data analytics, machine learning, and process automation into their Kaizen activities. Organizations can also increase efficiency, productivity, and competitiveness by using digital tools to automate repetitive work, streamline processes, and remove waste. This will help them accomplish their strategic goals more quickly and effectively.

Adopting a culture of learning and experimenting, empowering staff, utilizing technology, and accepting change are all valuable tactics for developing and modifying Kaizen methods. Accepting change entails seeing it as a necessary transition that presents a chance for development and innovation. Organizations can motivate staff members to experiment, explore new concepts, take measured risks, and learn from mistakes by establishing a culture of learning and experimenting. Giving workers the freedom, tools, and assistance required to effect significant change and drive positive change is critical to employee empowerment. Organizations can also foster productivity, efficiency, and innovation by utilizing technology to automate repetitive operations, optimize workflows, and enhance decision-making. This allows them to accomplish their strategic goals with more effectiveness and efficiency.

In today's dynamic and rapidly shifting business world, businesses that want to promote continuous improvement and achieve sustained success must adapt and evolve their Kaizen processes. Organizations may lead good change and stay ahead of the curve by embracing change, using technology, empowering employees, and promoting a culture of learning and experimentation. Furthermore, by adapting and evolving Kaizen techniques, organizations may better use the potential of creativity and innovation, encourage employee participation and ownership, and accomplish their strategic goals with greater effectiveness and efficiency. Ultimately, businesses can seize fresh chances, overcome obstacles, and go farther in their journey toward continuous improvement by embracing adaptation and evolution.

CHAPTER XII

Maintaining Momentum

Keeping the Kaizen Mindset Alive Long-Term

For people and businesses looking for long-term success and expansion, it is imperative to maintain the Kaizen mindset. The Kaizen philosophy, which has its roots in the Japanese idea of continuous development, stresses that significant advancements are often made by making tiny, gradual adjustments over time. But long-term retention of this mindset calls for commitment to continuous learning and development, persistence and dedication. This post will examine methods for preserving the Kaizen attitude throughout time, such as encouraging a constant improvement culture, adopting a growth mindset, establishing and modifying goals, developing resilience in the face of difficulties, and using feedback and reflection.

Long-term organizational adoption of the Kaizen attitude requires cultivating a culture of continual improvement. This entails fostering an atmosphere where workers are motivated to look for opportunities for development and creativity, exchange thoughts and opinions, and work together on projects to solve problems. Organizations can foster a sense of accountability and ownership within their workforce by encouraging open communication, transparency, and empowerment. This will lead to continual improvement across the board. Furthermore, highlighting achievements, praising staff members for their work, and offering training and development opportunities can all emphasize the Kaizen mentality's value and inspire people to keep aiming for perfection.

Maintaining the Kaizen mindset over time also requires adopting a growth mindset. The idea that skills and intelligence may be developed via commitment and work distinguishes a growth mindset from a fixed mindset. People with a growth mentality are better able to handle setbacks, are more willing to ask for feedback and educational opportunities, and are more open to change and innovation. Organizations may promote a culture of continuous learning and improvement, which will drive creativity and adaptation in a business environment that is constantly changing by helping executives and staff adopt a growth mindset.

Establishing and modifying objectives is another crucial tactic for maintaining the Kaizen attitude. Though the Kaizen philosophy strongly emphasizes achieving little, gradual changes, these efforts must also be guided by specific aims and objectives. Individuals and organizations can concentrate their efforts and monitor their progress over time by creating SMART goals—specific, measurable, achievable, relevant, and time-bound. But it's also critical to periodically evaluate and adjust goals in light of evolving situations, input, and lessons discovered. Goal-setting requires flexibility and adaptability, but individuals and organizations can ensure they always aim for development and progress.

Maintaining the Kaizen attitude over time also requires cultivating resilience in adversity. There will unavoidably be challenges and roadblocks in the path of ongoing progress. But in the end, what matters is how people and organizations handle these difficulties and continue to have a Kaizen attitude in the long run. Resilience is the capacity to withstand adversity, adjust to change, and push through obstacles toto emerge from adversity more robust and determined. It may be fostered in both individuals and organizations. Resilience-building techniques include keeping an optimistic mindset, asking for help when needed, taking lessons from mistakes, and concentrating on finding solutions rather than problems.

Moreover, sustaining the Kaizen mentality over time requires making the most of reflection and feedback. Feedback offers insightful information about areas that need work and growth prospects. Individuals and organizations can find places for development and obtain a deeper understanding of their strengths and limitations by proactively soliciting feedback from mentors, customers, and coworkers. Furthermore, making time for introspection—through journaling, meditation, or other contemplative activities—enables people to evaluate their development, recognize their accomplishments, and pinpoint areas where they still need to grow. Individuals and organizations may ensure they are constantly developing and expanding per the Kaizen principles by introducing feedback and reflection into everyday routines.

In conclusion, maintaining the Kaizen attitude over the long term takes commitment, tenacity, and a dedication to continuous learning and improvement. A growth mindset, goal-setting, goal-revising, building resilience in the face of adversity, and utilizing feedback and reflection are some ways that people and organizations can ensure that they are always aiming for excellence and promoting long-term success and growth. The benefits of continual improvement, such as higher productivity, creativity, and satisfaction, make the path worthwhile despite the obstacles. In a constantly changing world, people and organizations can realize their full potential and find long-term success by adhering to the Kaizen attitude.

Building a Supportive Community

Creating a supportive community encourages individual and group cooperation, development, and well-being. Communities—whether in online forums, local neighborhoods, or workplaces—are essential for fostering a sense of connection, belonging, and support among members. This section will discuss the importance of creating a supportive community, the components that make it successful, and methods for fostering and maintaining these kinds of groups.

A supportive community is fundamentally based on inclusivity, empathy, and trust. People feel appreciated, respected, and understood regardless of their circumstances, backgrounds, or views. People who live in a supportive environment take the time to actively listen to one another, provide support and encouragement, and acknowledge each other's accomplishments. Communities may establish a secure and inviting environment where people feel empowered to be honest and follow their goals and dreams by cultivating a culture of love, compassion, and acceptance.

Solid interpersonal ties are one of the most critical components of a supportive community. Real connections with people, frequent contacts, and shared experiences are the foundation of these relationships. Supportive community members establish relationships via reciprocity, empathy, and respect. They celebrate life's little victories and landmarks, offer emotional support to one another through trying times, and offer helpful criticism and direction when required. These connections support the cohesiveness and resiliency of the community as a whole and improve people's general well-being.

Another crucial element of a community that is supportive is effective communication. Members who communicate with clarity, openness, and honesty are more likely to trust one another and work together. Supportive group members can freely share their ideas, emotions, and worries without worrying about criticism or backlash. They actively listen to one another, try to comprehend various viewpoints, and collaborate to discover solutions to their problems. Through consistent communication channels, such as online forums, social media platforms, or regular gatherings, communities can foster discussion, idea sharing, and consensus building around shared goals and objectives.

Additionally, a nurturing community offers chances for both professional and personal development. Members can broaden their networks, learn new things, and develop talents through workshops, coaching, and mentoring. Communities can also provide resources and assistance to members to help them overcome roadblocks and hurdles to achievement. By providing educational possibilities, financial aid, or networking, communities can enable individuals to reach their maximum potential and confidently and resiliently pursue their goals.

Furthermore, a culture of cooperation and group effort is promoted by a supportive community. Members collaborate to address issues, find solutions, and bring constructive change to their communities. By combining their resources, skills, and knowledge, members can accomplish goals that would be challenging or impossible to reach independently. Communities have the power to significantly improve the lives of their constituents and the larger society, whether via grassroots initiatives, community service programs, or advocacy activities.

Diversity, equity, and inclusion are valued in a supportive community with solid interpersonal ties and efficient communication. It acknowledges and appreciates its members' diversity of backgrounds, experiences, and viewpoints. It works hard to foster an atmosphere where everyone feels important, welcomed, and empowered to engage fully. Communities may leverage their members' pooled wisdom, creativity, and ingenuity to drive good change and growth by embracing diversity and cultivating an inclusive culture.

In addition, a supportive community is flexible and sensitive to its constituents' changing needs and preferences. It conducts assessments, asks for feedback regularly, and modifies its services and activities to serve its members better. Communities aggressively seek member input through surveys, focus groups, and town hall meetings, using that information to guide planning and decision-making procedures. Communities may ensure that they continue offering their members pertinent and significant support over time by being adaptable and responsive.

In summary, creating a supportive community is crucial to encouraging individual and group cooperation, development, and well-being. Communities can create a safe and welcoming environment where members feel valued, supported, and empowered to thrive by fostering strong interpersonal relationships, effective communication, opportunities for personal and professional development, a culture of collaboration, diversity, equity, and inclusion, as well as flexibility and responsiveness. Communities can significantly improve the lives of their constituents and society by working together and demonstrating a shared commitment to change and prosper for future generations.

Personal Stories of Transformation through Kaizen

Narratives of individual metamorphoses via Kaizen provide compelling evidence of the potency of the continuous improvement ideology in promoting personal development, adaptability, and contentment. Through the continual application of Kaizen concepts, these stories provide insights into self-discovery, overcoming obstacles, and reaching personal and professional goals. This section will examine a range of individual narratives that demonstrate the transforming power of Kaizen, emphasizing the difficulties encountered, the tactics used, and the results attained by those who have adopted the Kaizen attitude.

One such tale is that of Sarah, a marketing expert who battled with work-life balance and time management.

Sarah was often stressed and couldn't fulfill deadlines since she felt overburdened by her work and personal obligations. After being frustrated with her lack of progress, she incorporated Kaizen's ideas into her everyday practice. Rather than attempting to implement significant changes simultaneously, Sarah concentrated on achieving tiny, gradual daily gains. She began by sorting her duties into priorities, establishing reasonable objectives, and breaking them into doable chunks. Sarah saw a noticeable increase in overall well-being, productivity, and efficiency over time. Sarah found that using a Kaizen approach to time management could better balance her job and personal life, recover control over her schedule, and experience less stress.

David's tale, a software developer who battled imposter syndrome and self-doubt, is another motivational one. Even with his technological know-how and proficiency, David frequently harbored self-doubt and worried about being discovered as a fraud. With a resolve to transcend his self-limiting thoughts, David sought advice from Kaizen. He started by questioning his pessimistic ideas and substituting them with uplifting statements. In addition, he actively sought out opportunities for growth and learning, such as attending networking gatherings and workshops, and he asked mentors and coworkers for input. With persistent work and dedication, David eventually became more self-assured and accepted his position as an essential team player. David overcame his fears and realized his full potential as a software engineer by using Kaizen principles in his career and personal growth.

In a similar vein, Maria's tale demonstrates the transformational potential of Kaizen in overcoming hardship and realizing objectives. After several personal and professional failures, Maria felt confused and unsure of her future, including a tough breakup and money problems. She looked to Kaizen for inspiration, determined to change her life. Maria concentrated on making tiny, constructive progress toward her daily objectives rather than obsessing about past mistakes. She broke down her ambitions into doable actions and gave herself specific, achievable goals, including getting a new career and getting her finances in better shape. Maria could restore her self-worth, find her purpose again, and construct a better future by gradually progressing. Maria's life changed from hopelessness and uncertainty to fulfillment and optimism because of the power of Kaizen.

John's narrative also demonstrates the transformational power of Kaizen in overcoming obstacles and realizing personal development. John had just graduated from college and was having trouble breaking through in the cutthroat employment market. He attended a great deal of interviews and sent out a great deal of resumes, but he kept getting rejected and lost faith in his skills. John, determined to keep going, looked to Kaizen for advice. He began by considering his advantages and disadvantages and his development opportunities. He then gave himself clear, attainable objectives, like sharpening his interviewing techniques and growing his professional network. John eventually achieved his desired job by performing tiny, regular daily acts, like attending networking events and rehearsing practice interviews. This helped him build confidence over time. John proved that persistence and commitment can result in success by overcoming hardship and achieving his goals through the power of Kaizen.

Apart from these individual accounts, corporations have achieved remarkable success and growth by implementing Kaizen concepts in several instances. For example, because of its dedication to innovation and ongoing improvement, the Japanese carmaker Toyota has come to be associated with Kaizen. Toyota has seen notable productivity, quality, and cost-effectiveness improvements by giving employees at all levels the freedom to find and fix process inefficiencies. Comparably, the Kaizen principles have been applied by Virginia Mason Medical Center in Seattle,

Washington, to enhance patient safety and care quality, leading to a notable decrease in medical errors and better patient outcomes. These illustrations show how Kaizen's transformational potential affects not just individuals but also organizations and entire industries, underscoring its enduring influence and broad applicability.

In conclusion, individual tales of change by Kaizen demonstrate the significant influence that the continuous improvement concept may have on people's lives. Through conquering obstacles, self-limiting ideas, and reaching personal and professional objectives, Kaizen enables people to take charge of their lives and effect good change. The concepts of Kaizen provide a path for development, adaptability, and fulfillment—whether through little, gradual adjustments to everyday activities or more significant changes to company culture. People can realize their full potential and design a life filled with opportunity, passion, and purpose by adopting the Kaizen attitude and committing to continuous learning and development.

CONCLUSION

The comprehensive manual "Kaizen Mindset: Transform Your Life with the Power of Continuous Improvement" offers guidance on implementing the concepts of Kaizen to attain personal and professional development. This book explores the idea of continual improvement, emphasizing its Japanese cultural foundations and wide range of practical applications. By adopting the Kaizen mentality, readers can learn to create little, constructive adjustments that add to significant, long-term changes. Through valuable examples, doable tactics, and perceptive case studies, the book illustrates how modest, continuous efforts can significantly improve overall well-being, productivity, and efficiency. "Kaizen Mindset" offers the resources and motivation to start this life-changing adventure, whether your goals are to advance your profession, improve your daily routines, or promote a continuous improvement culture inside your company. The book's focus on growth and mindset emphasizes the value of taking a proactive, upbeat approach to problems and encourages readers to see setbacks as chances for personal improvement. "Kaizen Mindset" is, in essence, a design for a happy, continuously changing existence rather than just a manual for self-improvement.

Thank you for buying and reading/ listening to our book. If you found this book useful/ helpful please take a few minutes and leave a review on the platform where you purchased our book. Your feedback matters greatly to us.